A COMPARATIVE ANALYSIS
OF CAPITAL PUNISHMENT

A COMPARATIVE ANALYSIS OF CAPITAL PUNISHMENT

Statutes, Policies, Frequencies, and Public Attitudes the World Over

Rita J. Simon and Dagny A. Blaskovich

LEXINGTON BOOKS

A division of
ROWMAN & LITTLEFIELD PUBLISHERS, INC.
Lanham • Boulder • New York • Toronto • Plymouth, UK

LEXINGTON BOOKS

A division of Rowman & Littlefield Publishers, Inc.
A wholly owned subsidary of The Rowman & Littlefield Publishing Group, Inc.
4501 Forbes Boulevard, Suite 200
Lanham, MD 20706

Estover Road
Plymouth PL6 7PY
United Kingdom

British Library Cataloguing in Publication Information Available

The hardback edition of this book was previously cataloged by the Library of Congress
as follows:

Simon, Rita James
   A comparative analysis of capital punishment : statutes, policies, frequencies,
and public attitudes the world over / Rita J. Simon and Dagny A. Blaskovich.
       p. cm.
   Includes bibliographical references and index.
   1. Capital punishment. 2. Comparative law. 3. Capital punishment—
Public opinion. I. Blaskovich, Dagny A., 1975– II. Title.
   HV8694 S55 2002
   364.66—dc21

                                    2002005659

ISBN-13: 978-0-7391-0382-1 (cloth : alk. paper)
ISBN-10: 0-7391-0382-2 (cloth : alk. paper)
ISBN-13: 978-0-7391-2091-0 (pbk : alk. paper)
ISBN-10: 0-7391-2091-3 (pbk : alk. paper)

Printed in the United States of America

♾™ The paper used in this publication meets the minimum requirements of American
National Standard for Information Sciences—Permanence of Paper for Printed Library
Materials, ANSI/NISO Z39.48–1992.

Contents

Tables

Preface

A COMPARATIVE ANALYSIS OF CAPITAL PUNISHMENT provides a brief history of the extent of the use of the penalty from ancient to modern time and examines the position of the major religions (Judaism, Christianity, Islam, Buddhism, and Hinduism) vis à vis capital punishment. This volume also reports the dates various countries in the world have abolished capital punishment and specifies the types of offenses for which various countries continue to employ the death penalty. It also reports the particular forms the penalty assumes (e.g., injection, firing squad, electrocution, and hanging) and the categories of persons who are exempt from the punishment (e.g., minors, the mentally ill, the mentally retarded, and pregnant women). The degree of public support, as reflected in national poll data for or against capital punishment, is also reported on a country-by-country basis.

Subsequent chapters look at data on whether the death penalty serves as an effective deterrent to violent offenders, especially homicide, to what extent innocent persons become victims of capital punishment, as well as the role DNA evidence has played in reducing those numbers. Also included is a chapter on genocide and democide, which reports the number of persons killed by their own government, especially in the twentieth century. The particular groups who have been targets of these mass killings are described in some detail.

A Comparative Analysis of Capital Punishment is the third in a series of volumes that examines a major public policy issue using an explicitly comparative approach. The organizing focus of the series is the analysis of important social issues about which many societies in the world have enacted laws and statutes, and about which most of its members have opinions that they voice in the public arena. They are issues that receive extensive media coverage as well as judicial attention. The first volume focused on abortion; the second on euthanasia. Subsequent topics may include marriage and divorce, drugs, and citizenship. Each volume should serve as a handbook containing empirical data and comprehensive references on the social issue or practice in question.

Rita J. Simon

Introduction

INFORMATION ON THE CRIMES for which the death penalty is imposed is as old as the earliest criminal codes. In *Story of Punishment: A Record of Man's Inhumanity*, Harry Elmer Barnes writes that the "origins of the death penalty rested primarily upon the effort to placate the gods, lest their beneficent solicitude for the group be diverted as a result of apparent group indifference to the violation of the social codes supposedly revealed by the gods of the people. The complete blotting out of the culprit was looked upon as a peculiarly forceful demonstration of groups' disapproval of the particular type of antisocial conduct involved in the case."[1]

The codes of the Babylonian King Hammurabi, issued around 1700 BCE, contained 27 clauses that applied capital punishment to a variety of crimes, including homicide. One example of a case that would result in the death penalty involves the following scenario. If a builder built a house for a man and did not make it strong enough, and the house collapsed and thereby caused the death of the man for whom it was built, the builder would be put to death. If the collapse resulted in the death of the son of the owner of the house, then the builder's son was put to death.[2]

Mosaic Law, which governed the Kingdoms of Judah and Israel up to 70 AD, when the Romans destroyed the Second Temple and conquered Jerusalem, defined 36 crimes for which the perpetrator would receive the death penalty. The crimes were divided into the following six categories:

1. Moral abuses, of which there were 18 types, including adultery, incest, relations between persons of the same sex;

2. Violations of religious laws, of which there were 12 types, including blasphemy, idolatry, false prophecy, witchcraft, profanation of the Sabbath;
3. Crimes against parents, of which there were three types;
4. Assault and Murder;
5. Kidnapping and selling into slavery;
6. Treason.

The forms that capital punishment took included stoning, which was the most common, burning, and decapitation. The last was reserved for persons who committed murder and communal apostasy.

In Ancient Greek society from 750 to 650 BCE, the death penalty was reserved for murderers and offenders against the state. The forms it took were by stoning or poison. Later, around 400 BCE, the death penalty was mandatory for robbing, embezzlement, and adultery, in addition to murder and treason. In addition to stoning and poisoning, other forms of capital punishment involved beating to death, hurling the perpetrator from a high rock or tower into a chasm, and placing him in a rock chasm that was fitted with spikes and hooks that were designed to tear and lacerate the body.

Ancient Roman law, which was available in written form in about 450 BCE, contained the Twelve Tables. The basic purpose of the Twelve Tables was to provide legal protection for the average citizen against the arbitrariness of the patricians in the judicial process. The Twelve Tables imposed the death penalty against judges who accepted bribes and against persons who bore false witness. The death penalty was also imposed on persons who committed arson, night theft, and exorcisms, the purpose of which was to make a person's crop sterile. In the first century BCE, the death penalty was imposed for political crimes committed by persons of the lower class. During the last stage of the empire, when Christianity became the state religion, heretics were frequently condemned and executed. The Code of Theodosius (438 AD) specified 80 crimes that were punishable by death.

In Ancient India, Brahmans who committed heinous crimes, including murder but excluding treason, would not be put to death. They would be banished and allowed to keep their wealth. Punishments, except for treason, where the death penalty was automatic for everyone generally depended on one's social status.

In China, capital punishment was imposed on priests who committed treason and persons who committed homicide, adultery, treason, witchcraft, incest, black magic, forgery, and theft of an object of substantial value. The husband of an adulterous wife was entitled to put his wife and her lover to death. Beating, burning, drowning, cutting to pieces, hanging, and throwing off a cliff were ways in which the death penalty could be enacted.

Shari'a, or Islamic law, formulated around 650 AD, divided crimes that were punishable by death into *Hudoud* crimes that were punishable by God—and included adultery and other forms of unlawful intercourse, highway robbery, murder (murder alone was not a death penalty crime)—and apostasy from Islam. Punishments that were determined by secular authority and for which the death penalty could be invoked were espionage and willful homicide. The forms in which the death penalty was enacted included stoning, flogging, and beheading.

Early Japanese criminal law is distinctive in that the death penalty was abolished for all crimes from 810 to 1157. No other society up to that time had abolished the death penalty for such a long period. In the beginning of the eighth century, the Japanese penal system was an imitation of the Chinese system. The death penalty was imposed for treason, rebellion, murder, night attack, burglary, and piracy. The penalty was enacted by crucifixion, burning at the stake, body in a cauldron, and beheading.

From the fall of the Roman Empire until the beginning of the modern era, capital punishment was widely practiced in Western Europe, most often by burning, beheading, and hanging. In the Middle Ages, mutilation of the offender was frequently employed. One reason for the widespread use of the death penalty in preindustrial societies was the lack of feasible alternatives. Imprisonment on a long-term basis was too expensive.

In thirteenth century England, death was the punishment for all felonies except mayhem and petty larceny. The most extensive use of capital punishment occurred in Western Europe during the onset of the industrial revolution, which produced a great deal of social dislocation and unrest that resulted in increased serious criminality. Sir William Blackstone, who wrote in the mid-eighteenth century, estimated that 160 crimes were punishable by death in England. A half-century later, probably another 100 were added. At the beginning of the nineteenth century, there were 200 capital crimes. By 1861, there were four: high treason, murder, piracy with violence, and destruction of dockyards. It was not until the nineteenth century that long-term imprisonment developed as a feasible alternative to the death penalty.

The death penalty was brought to North America by the colonizing powers, and in the American colonies it was used for many offenses. In British India, in the latter part of the nineteenth and twentieth centuries, murder and waging war against the king were capital offenses. The Canadian Criminal Code of 1892 provided the death penalty for treason, murder, rape, and piracy with violence. In British South Africa, treason, murder, and rape were considered capital offenses. Australia and elsewhere in the British Empire, murder and piracy with violence were capital offenses.

The movement to abolish capital punishment was initiated by Cesare Bone-sava, Marquis of Beccaria (1748–1794). His ideas were adopted by Jeremy Bentham (1748–1832), who persuaded Sir Samuel Romilly (1757–1818) to introduce a proposal in the British Parliament to abolish the death penalty. Portugal was the first country in Western Europe to abolish the death penalty for civil crimes, in 1867.

In the chapters that follow we describe the countries that have retained the death penalty by type of offense and those that have abolished the death penalty up to the time of writing. Data are reported by country on the frequency of use of the death penalty, the manner in which it is inflicted, and public attitudes toward its retention and abolition. Included also is a chapter on genocide (murder of minorities by the state) and democide (murder of the general population) mostly in the twentieth century.

Notes

1. Harry Elmer Barnes, *Story of Punishment: A Record of Man's Inhumanity* (Patterson Smith Publishing Corporation, 1996).

2. Israel Drapkin, *Crime and Punishment in the Ancient World* (Lexington Books, 1986), 26.

1

Religion and the Death Penalty

S INCE THE BIRTH OF THE FIRST RELIGION and the founding of the first civiliza-
tion, the death penalty has been a controversial issue. From Judaism,
Christianity, Islam, Buddhism, and Hinduism, the issue of the morality of the
death penalty has been discussed within each religion and continues to raise
legitimacy questions today.

Judaism

Judaism, founded on biblical and Mosaic law of the Old Testament and the
Torah, has had a wide range of applications of the death penalty. The religion
is based on a strong fear of and reverence for God, but strict interpretations of
the Bible have given credence to the support of the death penalty. The interpretation of the biblical concept holds the word of God as law. Therefore, following the "words of God" will ensure the well-being and prosperity of the individual, as well as the community as a whole. But the divination of the author
of the "laws" changes "crimes" into "sins," ultimately causing a violation of the
will of God if a "law" is broken.[1] Of all crimes, crimes or sins against another
human are deemed the most heinous because a human is made in the image
of God, *imago Dei*. The punishment, according to biblical law, is death if a
homicide is committed.[2]

Biblical law, which is based on Judaism, is not similar to the other ancient
laws, such as those of Mesopotamia or Sumeria. The *imago Dei*, unique to biblical law, creates an added emphasis to the crime of homicide, which is lacking

in the other nonbiblical laws. Vicarious punishment is another example of what was not acceptable under biblical law. Only the individual who committed the crime could be held accountable for the crime; family members and friends could not. Biblical law specifically prohibits "collective punishments:" "Parents shall not be put to death for children, not children for parents; only for their own crimes may persons be put to death" (Deut. 24:16).[3]

Biblical laws divided crimes into seven categories with corresponding punishments, which consisted of death, *karet* ("extirpation"), banishment, flagellation, *lex talionis*, fines, and penal slavery. Each method is described in detail within the Bible, except for flagellation, which is mentioned only vaguely in Deuteronomy. In Jerusalem, a special court system was established to try death penalty cases. A higher court was comprised of 23 judges selected from among the elders of the cities with populations of more than 120 families. The court was located at the gates of the city.[4]

The Jewish penal system is based on three distinctive characteristics: retributive, deterrent, and expiatory. The death penalty easily fits into these characteristics. In both Exodus and Deuteronomy, the Bible states that "an eye for an eye, and tooth for tooth" should be extracted when a crime has been committed. This principle, however, is not based in Jewish law, but is a derivation of Babylonian culture that was very influential in shaping early Hebrew life. Vengeance is not the foundation of this principle, but instead it was seen as an aid to reducing revenge from the family of the victim. Not only was the punishment equal, but it was swift and effective. No trial was necessary because there was already a law determining the punishment, a law from God.[5]

The deterrent characteristic appears in Deuteronomy 13:11: "Then all Israel shall hear and be afraid, and never again do any such wickedness."[6] The deterrent characteristic was more effective in ancient times because the punishment was not differentiated between the rich and the poor; it was universally applied to all who committed capital crimes.[7]

The last characteristic, the expiatory character, is illustrated in the crime of murder. The only punishment that would expiate such a crime as murder is death, because murder, especially willful murder, is an act against God. The fear of God and his wrath is at the heart of the Jewish religion, and therefore the act of expiation is very important. If the sin is not atoned for, the entire community may suffer at the hands of God. Therefore, even when the murderer is unknown, the elders of the city atone for the sin committed in order to supplicate the death of the member.[8] This is just one of the inconsistencies that appear within any religion when integrated into the criminal justice system of a country. Here the inconsistency is that while God has previously stated no other should be held accountable or punished for the acts of one man, the elders must atone for the sins of one man in order to appease God. This is not the only inconsistency that occurs in Judaism. In fact, conflicting statements are made throughout all of the religions in some form or fashion.

There are 36 capital crimes within the Mosaic law, divided into 6 categories: 18 moral abuses, 12 violations of religious laws, 3 types of crimes against parents, 1 crime of assault and murder, 1 type of forcible abduction and selling into slavery, and 1 type of treason. Three types of punishments for capital crimes are specified in the Mosaic law in order from least severe to most: decapitation, burning, and stoning.[9]

Stoning is the most frequently mentioned method of execution in the Bible and was considered the most severe. Eighteen of the thirty-six crimes were punishable by stoning. The location for the execution originally was outside the town, but was moved to the gates of the city, the place of the courts. The Bible appears to appoint the community as the executioner along with those who testified against the convicted individual. This role of the witnesses encourages accountability of the conviction and attempts to provide honest testimony from witnesses.[10]

Burning was the second most severe method of execution. Ten crimes were punishable by burning. There are no mentions of this type of execution anywhere in the Bible. But the postbiblical method for execution consisted of strangulation until the individual opened his mouth and molten lead was poured down his throat in order to burn the intestines. This technique was considered more humane and less painful; usually the individual was dead before the lead was poured. This method also preserved the body for burial.[11]

The final method of execution, which was deemed the least severe, was decapitation. It was considered quick and painless and was applied only to the willful murderer and those convicted of communal apostasy. In the Jewish system, it was necessary to prove intent because capital punishment was only possible when the murder was purposeful. The actual method of decapitation was an issue of dispute between the Amoraim and the Talmudists. Some Amoraim believed that the convicted should be standing while a sword was used to decapitate them. However, the Talmudists believed that the head could be placed on a block and cut off with an ax. They agreed, however, that at no time would a dagger be used or would an individual be cut in two with a sword. These methods were considered extreme and unnecessary.[12]

Whenever the Mosaic law failed to state the method of execution, strangulation was the method of choice. Crucifixion was not a method utilized by the Israelites; this method was primarily used by the Romans and was thought of as a method of deterrence. Jews believed crucifixion was a method that prolonged the agony of death. This method caused the individual to suffer for up to a day or more before death.[13] The methods utilized by the Jews had the characteristics of deterrence, but that was not a primary function of the death penalty and was never considered more important than the suffering of the convicted.

Christianity

Christianity was born out of Judaism. Their shared beliefs in the Old Testament established a foundation that is similar to Judaism, but their added beliefs stemming from the New Testament changes some Christians' belief in the ordained use of the death penalty. The Scriptures, though, can be used to support both sides of the death penalty argument. This dual interpretation has divided the Church since the early days of its founding. Those who opposed all forms of the death penalty have been in the minority, while even leaders of the church have been in support of this punishment. But today most major denominations oppose the death penalty and claim it to be "un-Christian."[14]

The argument for the death penalty stems primarily from the Old Testament. The belief that certain penalties are connected to certain crimes ordained by the word of God is the main point in the argument for the death penalty. But other tenets that are used in support of the death penalty include deterrence, protection of society, rehabilitation, and retribution. Even though the majority of the support relies on the retributive principle, Christians who support the death penalty believe that it is a moral imperative according to God's ordained order.

The primary moral argument based on Scriptures is of the *imago Dei*, or the image of God. This unique relationship between God and humans appears to be based on the belief that humans were made in the image of God, and if one should be murdered by another, than the only method of atonement for the sin is death. According to the Christian pro-death penalty groups, each person, whether they are a criminal or not, is made in the image of God, and they should then be treated with dignity and worth. A punishment that degrades the individual is, therefore, immoral. The question then becomes, does capital punishment degrade the individual? First, they believe that rehabilitation without the consent of the individual is more inhuman and degrading than the death penalty because "to punish criminals because they 'deserve' it is to respect them as morally responsible persons created in God's image who knew better and therefore have earned this punishment."[15]

Second, the concept of capital punishment is not in conflict with the image of God because capital punishment has been ordained by God in the Old Testament. The death penalty was established in order to protect the other "image bearers" from the one who destroys that image. God created capital punishment in order to respect human dignity, therefore it must be moral to utilize it. Human life is valued through the implementation and utilization of the death penalty. It provides an equal punishment for a heinous crime, while supporting a "pro-human" stance.[16]

The next argument in favor of the death penalty through the support of the Scriptures is that while it appears capital punishment is in opposition to the Sixth Commandment, it is not, because of the difference between private and public morality. The government has the ability to commit acts that a private citizen cannot; the death penalty is an example of that ability. A biblical example of this is when God ordered Israel to engage in warfare with the Canaanite tribes. The army was God's tool against the sinful tribes.[17] A general passage regarding the power of governments occurs in Romans 13:1: "Let every person be subject to the governing authorities; for there is no authority except from God, and those authorities that exist have been instituted by God."[18] Therefore to argue against the death penalty, a prescribed death, is to argue against the word of God; "Beloved, never avenge yourselves, but leave room for the wrath of God; for it is written, 'Vengeance is mine, I will repay, says the Lord.'"[19]

Another example of the power of the community over the power of the individual appears in Deuteronomy 21:18–21, where parents bring their children to the community for punishment when they have sinned:

> If someone has a stubborn and rebellious son who will not obey his father and mother, who does not heed them when they discipline him, then his father and his mother shall take hold of him and bring him out to the elders of his town at the gate of that place. They shall say to the elders of his town, "This son of ours is stubborn and rebellious. He will not obey us. He is a glutton and a drunkard." Then all the men of the town shall stone him to death. So you shall purge the evil from your midst; and all Israel will hear, and be afraid.[20]

It is the job and responsibility of the community or government to punish the wicked and honor the good. If the parents had killed their son alone, murder would have been committed, and the Sixth Commandment would have been broken. But since it was the will of the government to stone this boy to death, it was also the will of God because God appointed the government to that power. "Acts of personal vengeance are condemned as murder, but acts of capital punishment, being sanctioned by the government, are proper."[21]

A current problem with the state of the death penalty in the United States is the application of it. Discrimination abounds within the judicial system, particularly when it comes to the implementation of capital punishment. Christians who support the death penalty do not see the problem lying in the existence of the penalty, but solely in the application of it. The concept was conceived and ordained by God, and therefore can not be wrong. According to Ernest van den Haag, "discrimination is irrelevant" to the moral question of capital punishment.[22] Morality is not based on the application of the penalty, but on the concept, and the concept is moral and just.

Another problem with the application of the death penalty, which is even more serious, is the execution of innocent people. In the Old Testament, the method of trial in a capital case was detailed, in order to reduce the chance of innocent people suffering at the hands of injustice. But there has always been the chance that innocent people will be put to death. This does not affect the morality of capital punishment in the minds of Christians who support the death penalty. Again the problem lies in the application, not the morality. In fact, the argument could be made regarding all forms of punishment; innocent men and women are convicted wrongly. Does that mean all punishment should be abandoned? Not likely, but it does mean the judicial system needs to be improved in order to reduce the number of innocents punished unjustly.[23]

There is an opposing view, also held by many Christians, that the death penalty is wrong and immoral, and it should be abolished. This argument focuses on the New Testament and the idea that Christ eliminated the need for retribution of any kind by dying for the sins of humankind. His death meant that people no longer had to fear the retribution of God's wrath.

Even in the Old Testament, there are conflicting statements made regarding God's true opinion of the death penalty and the atonement of sins through an "eye for an eye" rationality. After the first murder, Cain murdering his brother Abel, Cain was worried about the retribution of the society: "My punishment is greater than I can bear! Today you have driven me away from the soil, and I shall be hidden from your face; I shall be a fugitive and a wanderer on the earth, and anyone who meets me may kill me."[24] But God replied by promising Cain that no one would be able to kill him: "Then the Lord said to him, 'Not so! Whoever kills Cain will suffer a sevenfold vengeance.' And the Lord put a mark on Cain, so that no one who came upon him would kill him."[25] Therefore, it appears that God did not want any atonement to be made through the death of Cain. In addition, the idea that vengeance escalates violence appears later in Genesis, when Lamech, a descendent of Cain, kills someone: "I have killed a man for wounding me, a young man for striking me. If Cain is avenged sevenfold, truly Lamech seventy-sevenfold."[26] The spiraling escalation that follows an act of vengeance or revenge simply increases the death toll and, ultimately, is never complete.

The interpretation of the Scriptures is a difficult task to undertake. Each view can be supported in various passages throughout the Bible, and knowing what was intended when the words were written can be hard. For those who believe in the abolishment of the death penalty, the commandment made to Noah regarding the retaliation when a man is killed is not read as a law, but as a simple description of the way things are:

> Whoever sheds the blood of a human,
>   by a human shall that person's blood be shed;
> for in his own image God made humankind.[27]

There are six general reasons behind the use of vengeance as described in the Bible: eradication, imitation, intimidation or deterrence, retaliation, revenge, and expiation. Today, the majority of those who support the death penalty believe in its power of deterrence. This, though, does not have a strong connection to the Scriptures. The question becomes: "Is killing a killer a vengeful action against the evildoer himself? Or is it the restoration of divine moral balance through sacrifice?"[28] It appears to be more sacrificial than vengeful, and ultimately that sacrifice was made for all in the death of Jesus Christ. The shedding of his blood for the sins of all should eliminate any need for vengeance. In Genesis, though, this sacrifice had not yet been made, although those today who support the death penalty on the basis of the text that appears in Genesis and throughout the Old Testament are failing to grasp the dramatic change and sacrifice that is made in the New Testament.

While opposition to the death penalty utilizes passages from both the New Testament and the Old Testament, it is the New Testament that clearly distinguishes Judaism from Christianity. The belief that Christ was the savior is vital to the argument regarding capital punishment. The sacrificial rituals that occur throughout the Old Testament end with the ultimate sacrifice of Christ. His blood was shed so that others may be forgiven. The fact that this main tenet of Christian Scriptures is overlooked completely undermines the argument used by those who support the death penalty. Christians who oppose the death penalty clearly have the predominant argument because they analyze the Scriptures as a whole, not selectively. They are also able to provide a counterargument to the supporters' arguments.

One of the basic arguments that has been used by supporters of the death penalty is the "eye for an eye" passage that occurs three times in the Bible. The retaliatory God that appears throughout the Old Testament is replaced by a compassionate, forgiving God in the New Testament. The "eye for an eye" passage occurs in Exodus, Leviticus, and Deuteronomy. In Exodus, the passage is recited as poetry, a background for the situation when a woman is injured while two men are fighting. It is not seen as the primary passage, but as a secondary one that is more legal lore than fact. According to John Yoder, "it is recited as a celebration of the poetic fittingness of letting every punishment fit the crime, one more reminder of the ancient near eastern vision of deep cosmic symmetry, even though it is of no use for the present case. We note that *if* the rule is applied literally in this case, the death penalty is here to be imposed for an *accidental* killing."[29]

In Leviticus, a question is being posed to God as to the correct punishment for blasphemy. After being told that the individual should be stoned to death, the passage is repeated regarding the appropriate fittingness for punishment. But, again, this passage does not seem to be appropriate because it does not have anything to do with the question posed to God. Another problem with this passage is that the punishment does not seem to fit the crime; a man who curses at God should be cursed at by God, but instead is sentenced to death. This discrepancy does not appear to fit into the "eye for an eye" ideology that is used to defend the death penalty.[30] If the acts of God do not align with the words of God, it seems one should follow the acts and use them to interpret the true meaning of the words.

The same thing occurs in the passage in Deuteronomy. Here the passage formally contradicts the idea of retaliation. It is here that the rules of evidence required during the trial are laid out. The careful method of testifying and the harsh punishment for perjury show that blind revenge was not the motive behind the "eye for an eye" passages; instead it is meant only that their punishment should fit the crime. The punishment should be no greater than the crime committed.[31]

At no time is this frequently used passage the main message or subject of the Scripture. It always comes as a secondary message used to highlight the main subject. Also this discrepancy occurs every time this passage is used. Never does God follow the actual message to the letter. This failure should be seen as God's example of reality versus blind revenge. At no time does God take the retaliation out on an individual, at least not in the three passages utilizing the "eye for an eye" passage, which are commonly referred to by supporters of the death penalty.

It appears that the Christian Scriptures do not support the death penalty through the arguments utilized by those who support the punishment. While the death penalty is used as a form of punishment in the Bible, no clear logic seems to conform to provide a clear rationale for the use of the penalty. When the death of Christ is added to the previous Scriptures, the death penalty no longer becomes a viable method for punishment because of the purpose of Christ's death. It becomes evident after considerable examination of the Christian Scriptures that the death penalty is not supported by the Bible when the whole of the text is considered.

Islam

Islam, based on the teaching of Muhammad, is founded on the basic belief that one needs to surrender or submit oneself to the will of God. Islam builds on the Scriptures of the Old Testament, but the Koran takes the place of the Torah and the New Testament. The Koran is filled with utterances that are considered the literal word of God, and should be followed as such. Muhammad claimed to be the direct descendent of Abraham, a figure he claimed was neither Jew nor Christian. The basic tenets of the Islamic religion, which was founded in the seventh century, can be summarized as the "Five Pillars of Islam"—faith, prayer, alms-giving, fasting, and pilgrimage.[32] To become a Muslim, a person need only say *"la-ilaha illa Allah; Muhammadum rasull Allah."* After reciting this phrase in front of any Muslim, one then becomes a Muslim. There is no turning back after the recitation, for once you have become Muslim, to speak out against the religion is punishable by death.[33]

From the beginning, crimes and punishments appeared in the Shari'a, the Islamic law.[34] The Shari'a played a crucial role in stabilizing the legal norms and social order of Muslim countries.[35] According to the Shari'a, crime is "the commission of an act that is legally forbidden and punishable or the omission of a duty that is commanded. Crime is punishable in this world by fixed (*Hudoud*) or discretionary (*tazir*) punishments." In classical Islamic law, there is no distinction between religious crimes and secular crimes. Criminal laws are more developed within the Shari'a then they are in the civil code.[36]

There are five categories of offenses outlined and identified within the Shari'a: "(1) those with a specific punishment (*hadd*); (2) those for which the punishment is at the judge's discretion (*ta'zir*); (3) those describing talio or retaliatory action (*kisas*), inflicted by the victim's kinsmen, or blood money (*diya*), to be paid by the perpetrator or his kinsmen; (4) those against the policy of the state, deserving administrative penalties (*siyasa*); and (5) those that are corrected by acts of personal penance (*kaffara*, 'expiation')."[37] Basically, in a Muslim country, everything is seen as permissible unless it is specifically prohibited. Punishments under the *Hudoud* crimes are prescribed by God in the Koran and the Shari'a, and are immutable. Some of these specified punishments include death—death by stoning, sword, and crucifixion depending on the crime. *Ta'zir*, or discretionary punishments, is seen as the most important section because it contains the majority of the crimes committed. These crimes were seen as having deterrent or rehabilitative objectives. A secular authority determined the punishments, and therefore the punishments varied according to circumstances. But death is also an option for these offenses.[38]

Talio (*kisas*) or blood money (*diya*) contains the crime of homicide. Islamic law treated homicide as a crime somewhere between a tort and a crime, and therefore modified the punishments in three ways. First, blood feuds were abolished. Second, vengeance could be exacted only after a judicial proceeding to determine the guilt of the accused. And finally, punishment was sealed according to the degree of culpability and the harm inflicted on the victim.[39] There are three types of punishment that accompany the crime of homicide: retaliation, or talio; blood money; and, penitence. Under retaliation, death is the punishment as long as the victim's family throws the first stone or is present at the time of the execution. There are, however, instances when homicide is excusable. So while death is a possible punishment for homicide, it is not an absolute.[40]

Islamic law clearly supports the death penalty. Both the Koran and the Shari'a specifically identify various forms of execution as the method of punishment for certain offenses. Because of the lack of separation of religious and secular offenses, the Islamic law infiltrates the state law, creating a predominately religious atmosphere surrounding the criminal justice system. This connection to the religious makes any crime a crime against God, as well as man, and requires complete atonement within both spheres. The practical applications of Islamic law are seen in countries within the Middle East.

Buddhism

Buddhism originated in India in the sixth century BCE, but did not reach its peak until between the second century BCE and the second century CE. It may have been a reaction to the severity of the Brahmanic Age that proceeded it. Buddhism was born out of the teachings of a man named Siddhartha Guatama, who later became known as Buddha. The popularity of Buddhism may be attributed to a number of factors. First, Buddha taught in the vernacular as opposed to Sanskrit, thus making his teachings more available to a larger population. Second, Buddhism contained no elaborate rituals; anyone could follow its teachings if they had a strong self-discipline. Third, it was a religion without a god and without a proscribed system of worship. Fourth, Buddha's five moral views were widely and easily accepted because of their basic humanity and of their contribution to improving the relationship between all peoples. Fifth, Buddhism did not distinguish between castes. And finally, Buddhism was concerned with relieving the suffering for all people rather than emphasizing the differences between them.[41]

Buddhism was a major joining and civilizing force throughout Southeast Asia from the second to the ninth centuries. After the death of Siddhartha Guatama, his successors split his movement into sects—the Greater and Lesser Vehicles. The Greater Vehicle deified Buddha and created a complete cosmology with heavens and hells, as well as a religious ritual. All of the things created by the sects opposed all of Buddha's basic tenets. Of the many cults that did evolve from the basic Buddhism, Jainism is the only one to survive.[42]

Jainism was founded by a young man named Nataputta Vardhamana. The basic beliefs of Jainism were based on the idea of Karma and reincarnation, as well as the concept of the Brahma (the neutral and impersonal spirit) and Atman (the internal ego of every man), but redefined these terms. Jains believe that all creatures and objects have souls. Monks took special care when walking outside and breathing the air in order to prevent harming insects. Violence against any creature was absolutely forbidden. But they did take an unusual delight in death. Suicide by starvation was seen as the highest accomplishment an individual could achieve.[43]

Before the death of Buddha, he prescribed 227 rules to control criminal behavior through the establishment of certain punishments. During the Buddhist Age, though, confessions played an important role in determining punishments. After Buddha's death and the fracturing of his beliefs and initial tenets, confessions were usually extracted through torture. But individuals who confessed to their crime usually received lesser punishments. Punishment was never retaliatory; it was always meant to act as a method for cleansing the soul through mental or physical suffering.[44]

Buddhism also flourished in China and Japan. Each country, including India, developed differently primarily because of the pervasive divergences within each society.[45] In China, most of the original Buddhists were Taoists because of the similarity in beliefs between the two religions. These first believers appeared in the first century CE. There was a difference between Buddhism and Confucianism. In fact, the rise of Buddhism in China coincided with the decline of Confucianism during the six-dynasties period. The penal code in China developed independently from religion, but the effects of Buddhism on the severity of the punishments during its peak in China is obvious. The penal law in China was concerned predominately with retaining the social order, and a disruption in it was identical to a disruption in the cosmic order. But the death penalty did exist in China and was severe.[46]

Japan is the final country that was affected by the adoption of Buddhism into their religious order. Buddhism did not reach Japan until the sixth century. At the beginning of the eighth century, there were two methods for execution: hanging or beheading. The methods of execution were less severe in Japan perhaps due to the influence of Buddhism at that time.[47]

Buddhism is a religion based on the belief in peace and coexistence. It does not support the death penalty in any method or fashion because its basic tenet founded by Buddha was to provide a religion for all; a religion that attempted to deter crime and allow punishments that helped in the complete atonement for the crime. Atonement was not similar to Christianity, where the atonement was to God; this atonement was to the cosmos, the social and universal order of all.

Hinduism

Hinduism, also known as New-Brahmanism, followed Buddhism and Jainism in India. The basics of Buddhism and Jainism had all but disappeared in India, but they remained within the belief systems of the people, and led to the birth of Hinduism. This religion flourished between the second and ninth Centuries within India. It accommodated the primitive deities, as well as aspects of each of the predominate religions in India: "the philosophical speculations of the Brahmans; the nonviolence of Jainism; and, the ethics of Buddhism, which ignored the Indian caste system." Today, Hinduism has millions of gods, no fixed system of worship, no clergy, and no creed. There is also no founding father or prophet.[48]

The Hindu belief is based on three fundamental concepts: reincarnation, karma, and dharma. Karma is the law that judges all man's physical and spiritual actions. Dharma is the moral code that determines how one should live his or her life. Each man is bound by Dharma, and each man's Dharma is unique and based on his role in life. Unlike Buddhism, which was independent of the caste system, Hinduism is completely intertwined with India's caste, and even justifies the system.[49]

The Law of Manu, the basis for political government and justice in India, determined that the Brahmans, or priests, were the highest caste and, therefore, all of the universe belonged to them. To a large extent, the Law of Manu represents the Brahmans' ideal picture of what the law ought to be. It is hard to determine the exact time the laws were written. Scholars place them between 1280–880 BCE and believe they were passed orally until somewhere between the first century BC and fourth century CE, when they were written down.[50]

Crime is defined in these ancient scriptures as "an act contrary to either the divine code or the state laws."[51] Criminal behavior was seen as being linked to the moral conduct of one's daily life. Punishment was seen as a religious duty. Sins were punished by expiation, as ordained in the sacred books, where crimes were punished by sanctions determined by the king and the courts. The Law of Manu held that the state's most powerful tool of enforcement was force. They believed that punishment was a science and that it "indirectly brings about a natural tendency in the average individual to obey the law of the land, which renders the frequent use of force unnecessary. It ultimately secures proper progress in religion, philosophy, and economic well-being."[52]

The mind was seen as the main source of human behavior, and major consideration was given to the treatment of offenders when they repented for their sins. Any admission of guilt was greatly appreciated by the judge or king of the court and taken into account when sentencing the offender. Physical punishment was considered a last resort and then only used for heinous crimes. Usually, exile or other nonviolent punishment was preferred. This aversion to physical punishment could be attributed to the fact that punishment was the righteousness emanating from the divine right of the king and was based on four important principles: prevention, correction, purification, and, only lastly, eradication. Deterrence was also considered. The basic aim of punishment was to deter abnormal tendencies and transform them into healthy social urges for the benefit and safety of the society. Fear of pain was thought to constitute a large enough deterrent to crime.[53]

Unlike other judicial systems and religious beliefs, once the punishment had been completed by the individual or they had been pardoned, the sin of the crime was completely wiped away, and the individual was given a clean slate in life. Actually, a pardon from the king was the norm rather than the exception. In fact, pardoning was seen as the greatest virtue to be observed by all, because given certain circumstances, anybody could commit a crime.[54] Individualization of punishment was also a consideration: "punishment should be accorded to the merits of each case, after due consideration of the mind of the offender and the circumstances under which the offense was committed."[55] Kautilya, a Brahman who was known as the "Italian Macchiavelli," warned that if a punishment was too severe, it would alarm the people; if it was too mild, it would frustrate them; therefore the proper punishment was encouraged. For that purpose, a penal science had to be studied with regard to the past, present, and future, as well as taking into consideration the four orders of Indian society. The penal system had to be flexible in order to fit the crime, as well as the criminal.[56]

Capital offenses existed in ancient India, and the death penalty was utilized. The most common methods of execution consisted of fire, strangulation, hanging, drowning, crucifixion, decapitation, being torn apart by dogs, or being crushed by elephants. A convicted man had three days to pray for his soul and redemption, and thus win a place in the world-to-come. Besides treason, the punishment of death was dependent on the social class of the offender. While the death penalty was an option for punishment, it was not commonly used.[57]

Laws regarding crimes and punishments did not appear in India until the Brahmans began to have an interest in the country's administration. Until then, religion and morality were the topics of Indian literature. It was sufficient to live according to one basic philosophical principle: "Nobody causes happiness or misery to anyone. It is wrong to think that pain and pleasure had been caused by others. It is you alone and your actions which are responsible for both these conditions."[58]

The genius of India consists of synthesis. Successive cultural influences have fused together to form the intricate way of life we know as India and Hinduism. Even within such a limited subject as crime and punishment, Indians were the first to develop the notions of "negligence" and "judicial psychology."[59]

Hinduism, while allowing for the death penalty, does not seem to completely support it. The belief in reincarnation and karma influenced the judicial system through the increased support of confessions and pardons as methods of punishment. Hinduism's basic premise is based on living this life for the reward in the next. Capital punishment was seen as an excessive punishment; lesser punishments were seen as adequate enough to deter others from committing crimes.

Each religion has played a different role in the utilization of the death penalty, some more, some less. Judaism and Christianity have not played as prominent a role as Islam and Hinduism in shaping and affecting penal systems. Buddhism, while it was influential in some countries, was not continuous or permanent. Religion is global and has affected civilizations since the dawn of the first religion. It gives people a foundation of morality from which to build their lives and societies, their laws and punishments. While not all religions play a vital role in the direct shaping of a judicial system, they are critical in the molding of attitudes toward behaviors that are acceptable within a society, and this includes the utilization of the death penalty.

Notes

1. Drapkin, *Crime and Punishment,* 56.
2. House and Yoder, *The Death Penalty Debate: Issues of Christian Conscience* (Word Publishing, 1991), 73.
3. *Holy Bible,* Catholic edition.
4. Drapkin, *Crime and Punishment,* 60–62.
5. Ibid., 68.
6. Holy Bible, Catholic edition.
7. Drapkin, *Crime and Punishment,* 69.
8. Ibid.
9. Ibid., 70–71.
10. Ibid., 71.
11. Ibid., 73–74.
12. Ibid., 74.
13. Ibid.

14. House and Yoder, *Death Penalty Debate*, 5–6.
15. Ibid., 73.
16. Ibid., 74.
17. Ibid.
18. Holy Bible, Catholic edition.
19. Holy Bible, Catholic edition, Romans 12:19 citing Deuteronomy 32:35.
20. Holy Bible, Catholic edition.
21. House and Yoder, *Death Penalty Debate*, 76.
22. Ibid., 77.
23. Ibid., 78
24. *Holy Bible*, Catholic edition, Genesis 4:13–14.
25. Ibid., Genesis 4:15.
26. Ibid., Genesis 4:23–24.
27. Ibid., Genesis 9:6.
28. House and Yoder, *Death Penalty Debate*, 124–26.
29. Ibid., 134.
30. Ibid., 135.
31. Ibid.
32. Drapkin, *Crime and Punishment*, 254–55.
33. Ibid., 255.
34. Ibid., 276.
35. Ibid., 273.
36. Ibid., 276.
37. Ibid.
38. Ibid., 276–80.
39. Ibid., 281.
40. Ibid., 281–84.
41. Ibid., 108–9.
42. Ibid., 109.
43. Ibid.
44. Ibid., 122–23.
45. Ibid., 328.
46. Ibid., 147–49.
47. Ibid., 359.
48. Ibid., 110.
49. Ibid.
50. Ibid., 111.
51. Ibid., 119.
52. Arth. Chana. I:4.
53. Drapkin, *Crime and Punishment*, 127.
54. Ibid., 128.
55. Manu, VIII:126.
56. Drapkin, *Crime and Punishment*, 129.
57. Ibid., 129.
58. Ibid., 133.
59. Ibid.

2

Countries That Have Abolished
and Retained the Death Penalty

B Y THE END OF THE TWENTIETH CENTURY, more than half the countries in the world had abolished the death penalty in some form or fashion. As of September 2000, 87 countries still retained the penalty, 21 countries were considered "abolitionist de facto," 75 had abolished the penalty completely, and 12 countries retained the death penalty for crimes under military law or crimes committed during wartime.[1] In 1999, 85 percent of all executions reported occurred in only five countries: China, Iran, Saudi Arabia, the Democratic Republic of the Congo, and the United States.[2] Tables A.1 through A.5 located in the appendix provide detailed information on those countries that have abolished the death penalty for all crimes; those countries that have abolished the death penalty for ordinary crimes only; those countries which formally retain the death penalty for ordinary crimes, but may be considered abolitionist in practice because they have not executed anyone for at least the past ten years, or because they made an international commitment not to carry out executions; those 87 countries that retain and use the death penalty for ordinary crimes; and a breakdown of the countries that retain the death penalty and the types of offenses that are punishable by death.

Every year more than three countries abolish the death penalty for all crimes committed within their country.[3] The countries that do retain the death penalty, for the most part, are third world or communist countries. The exception is the United States of America. The United Nations and Amnesty International continue to attempt to pass laws and acts that would ultimately abolish the death penalty in every country. But the United States, and other select few, continue to vote against any bill that would restrict their ability to carry out death sentences.

There are three international treaties in existence today that have been adopted by a number of countries that promise not to have the death penalty within their country. These three treaties are: the Second Optional Protocol to the International Covenant on Civil and Political Rights, which has been ratified by 43 countries, with the promise of 5 more countries who will ratify it at a later date; Protocol No. 6 to the European Convention for the Protection of Human Rights and Fundamental Freedoms, ratified by 37 European states; and the Protocol to the American Convention on Human Rights to Abolish the Death Penalty, which has been ratified by 6 American countries and has been signed by 2. Protocol No. 6 calls for the abolishment of the death penalty in times of peace. The other two call for total abolishment of the death penalty, but allow the states to retain the penalty in times of war.[4]

The following sections describe the different countries' policies regarding the death penalty.

The United States of America, Canada, and Australia

The United States of America is unique because it is one of the only industrialized democratic nations to retain the death penalty. Not only does it retain the death penalty, but it uses it with great frequency. Within the United States, each state has been allowed to determine whether the death penalty will be a possible punishment for capital offenses. As of July 1, 2000, 40 jurisdictions retain the death penalty on their books. Only 13 jurisdictions have abolished the penalty for all crimes.[5] As of 2000, there were approximately 3,565 prisoners on death row in the United States. Ninety-eight people were executed in 1999, the highest number since 1954. The average time a condemned person spends between sentencing and execution is nine and a half years. There is also a discriminatory air regarding the use of the death penalty. While statistics show that a slightly higher percentage of the death row population is white, approximately 42 percent of the population is African American, which is largely disproportionate to the 13 percent of the general population they make up. The race of the victim also plays a role in the severity of the punishment. Historically, 80 percent of persons convicted of killing a white individual were sentenced to death, although a larger percentage of victims are African American.[6]

The United States is also distinct in that it has executed the highest rate of children and mentally retarded individuals. Since 1973, more than 160 children have been sentenced to die. This figure is greater than the other five countries that also allow children to be sentenced to death. Twelve states do not even have a minimum age set for imposing death. Since 1976, 31 mentally retarded inmates have been executed, 19 within the past five years. Over 300 death row inmates are expected to be mentally retarded, which means that approximately 10 percent of the inmates on death row are suffering some form of mental retardation.[7]

Canada and Australia both no longer retain the death penalty. Australia officially abolished the death penalty for ordinary crimes in 1984 and for all crimes in 1985. But their last known execution was in 1967. Canada officially abolished the death penalty for ordinary crimes in 1976 and for all crimes in 1998. Their last execution was in 1962. With the exception of a serious crime such as murder, it is common for an individual to serve four or five probationary terms before they are sentenced to prison. The Canadian focus is more on community-based corrections than on penitentiaries.[8]

Central and South America–Chile, Belize, and Colombia

The current situation in the Central and South American countries regarding the death penalty is tenuous, at best. Drugs and violence are rampant within most of these countries. While the death penalty is not always utilized or legal, torture and paramilitary groups control the level of unrest and violence below the radar of the legal system. Human rights are being violated in all three countries, not necessarily at the hands of legitimate power figures.

Chile's criminal justice system, today, retains the death penalty. But that was not always the case. In 1930, the death penalty was abolished, but was subsequently reinstated for certain crimes in 1937. Today, capital punishment can be imposed for more than 20 offenses, in both civil and military legislation. It has not been carried out recently; instead death sentences frequently have been commuted to life imprisonment. Since 1992, the parliament has been studying proposals to widen the scope of the use of capital punishment. Any attempt to abolish the death penalty has consistently been hindered by the senate.[9] A problem that exists in Chile is the number of deaths that occur while an individual is in custody. Torture of detainees has been reported to Amnesty International, despite the fact that torture is specifically prohibited in the Chilean constitution.[10]

Belize, similar to Chile, also retains the death penalty. But Belize is more apt to execute rather than commute death sentences. The method of execution is hanging. In April 1999, a constitutional question was posed to the Supreme Court: Does the death penalty constitute cruel and inhuman punishment? The Supreme Court ruled that death by hanging could not constitute cruel and inhuman punishment because the death penalty is sanctioned by the Belize constitution, and therefore could not be defined as cruel or inhuman. In 1999, there were eight prisoners on "death row," although there were no death sentences issued or carried out. The death penalty in Belize is issued for individuals convicted of criminal homicide, although death is not an automatic sentence. According to the constitution, the judge of record must submit a report to the Belize Advisory Council, which then advises the attorney general as to the appropriateness of the punishment.[11]

Colombia, while it no longer retains the death penalty, is guilty of forced disappearances, genocide, and massacres. The death penalty in Colombia is said to have aroused a good deal of opposition in the nineteenth century and was therefore abolished in 1910.[12] But the country is plagued by violence and "death squad"-style killings. In 1999, at least 150 people "disappeared" after being captured by paramilitary groups.[13] These paramilitary groups were declared illegal in 1989, but continue to terrorize and murder many innocent civilians and political leaders every year. Within the first ten months of 1987, death squads killed approximately 100 political leaders per month. While these statistics appear to be quite large, it was estimated that in 1987 nearly 80 percent of the crimes committed were not reported. And of the 20 percent reported, only 1 percent resulted in conviction and sentencing.[14] While Colombia does not have the death penalty on their books any longer, there are many other more vicious incidents which occur that most likely would not be affected by the implementation of the death penalty. Their crimes are committed by a subculture that is nearly impossible to control, much less capture, convict, and punish.

Western Europe–England/Wales, France, Germany, and Italy

On June 29, 1998, the countries in the European Union (EU) agreed that the death penalty should be abolished worldwide. The battle against the death penalty is an important aspect of the EU's human rights policy. In order to become a member of the EU, a state must never apply the penalty of death. Italy was the first country to take up this battle. It introduced a motion against the death penalty to the United Nations Commission for Human Rights in Geneva.[15] While the EU is battling for universal abolishment of the death penalty, one country in the EU still retains the death penalty, if in name only. England/Wales has not completely abolished the death penalty for all crimes. While the death penalty remains on their books, they abolished the punishment for ordinary crimes in 1973, and their last execution was in 1964.[16]

France, Germany, and Italy have abolished the death penalty for all crimes. The French penal codes in the past have greatly affected the tone of the penal codes in both Germany and Italy. The predominant sentiment of the penal code enacted in Germany was retribution, adopted from the French. Heavy emphasis was placed on the prevention of crime through punishment. But this has changed, and today the Germans consider general deterrents ineffective for individual punishment. They concentrate more on the rehabilitation of the individual, as well as the prevention of crime.[17] The last execution in the Federal Republic of Germany (FRG) was in 1949. The death penalty was officially abolished for all crimes in 1949, as well. The date of the last execution in the German Democratic Republic (GDR) is unknown. The death penalty in the GDR was officially abolished in 1987. In October 1990, the FRG was unified with the GDR.[18]

Italy also derived some of its penal ideologies from the French Enlightenment, although political philosophers such as Beccaria, Montesquieu, and Voltaire have also influenced the Italian penal codes. As stated earlier, Italy has taken the lead in the battle to end executions around the world. The last execution to occur in Italy was in 1947, which is also when it officially abolished the death penalty for ordinary crimes. Today the death penalty exists in military law, meaning it may be enacted in wartime.[19]

France was inspired by English law after the Revolution of 1789 with regard to the principle of legality of offenses and punishments. France has a rich history with the death penalty. The birth of the guillotine and the reign of terror are significant parts of French history. But France performed a radical transformation since the revolution, and today it no longer retains the death penalty on its books. The last execution that occurred in France was in 1977, and the death penalty was finally abolished for all crimes on October 9, 1981.[20] France, now a member of the EU, has joined the battle for universal abolishment of the death penalty.

Eastern Europe–Russia, Ukraine, Kazakhstan, Poland, Slovenia, and the Czech and Slovak Republics

Eastern Europe is rich in violent history. Russia has been the predominately influential country in this area. The former Soviet Union controlled much of Eastern Europe. Today, the former republics of the Soviet Union continue to retain the death penalty, while some of the non-Soviet countries abolished the death penalty shortly after the fall of the Soviet Union. Russia, today, continues to utilize the death penalty. The penalty may be imposed only for serious violent crimes against human life, according to the Constitution of 1993. During the early 1990s, the Russian Federation conducted 60 executions per year. The most common method utilized by the Russians for execution is the firing squad. The age of criminal responsibility is 16, but by the age of 14, an individual can be held accountable for his crimes if the crime is: murder, major bodily injury, rape, kidnapping, larceny, robbery, burglary, stealing of firearms, drugs, and malicious hooliganism. But the courts have the ability to impose educational or reform measures on individuals under the age of 18.[21] Since 1990, the Russian Federation has not executed any child offenders.[22]

The Ukraine, a former republic of the Soviet Union, declared independence in August 1991. It retained the death penalty even after their separation from the Soviet Union until recently. On March 22, 2000, the president of the Ukraine, Leonid Kudma, signed into law the abolishment of the death penalty. In December 1999, the Constitutional Court had deemed the death penalty a violation of human rights, and thus unconstitutional. It has been replaced by a sentence of life imprisonment. The Ukraine also ratified Protocol No. 6 to the European Convention on Human Rights.[23]

Prior to the March signing, the death sentence could be imposed on an offender for aggravated homicide, rape of a minor, treason, espionage, and certain military offenses. An individual under the age of 18 or a pregnant woman could not be executed. Individuals fitting these descriptions at either the time of the crime, at the time of sentencing, or at the time of execution could not receive the death penalty. During peacetime, the death penalty could be applied to other crimes, such as the assassination of a government or foreign official, sabotage, aggravated murder, and other military offenses.[24]

Kazakhstan, also a former republic of the Soviet Union, continues to retain the death penalty, even after the break up of the Soviet Union. In 1995, 110 death sentences were passed and 101 executions were carried out. Kazakhstan ranked fourth that year in the number of executions carried out worldwide. Relative to the size of this country, 101 executions in one year is very high. This number, however, has been reported by Amnesty International, while the official number reported by the Kazakhstani government is 63.[25]

Kazakhstan retains the death penalty for 18 peacetime offenses. Only 4 offenses have resulted in the death penalty being applied between 1987 and 1991, according to Amnesty International's statistics. They were murder under aggravating circumstances, rape, threatening the life of a police officer, and banditry. In 1995, the only offense that the death penalty was applied to was aggravated homicide. The punishment of death cannot be applied to an offender under the age of 18 at the time of the crime or a pregnant woman. The method used is "execution-style"—a single shot to the back of the head. On average the period of time between the sentencing phase and the execution is one year. That includes all attempts at clemency and appeal proceedings.[26] Between 1987 and 1990, a total of 165 sentences were handed down, but 41 of them were commuted or pardoned. In 1991, 67 death sentences were decreed and at least 26 were subsequently commuted.[27]

Poland has been in a transitional phase since the breakdown of the Communist system in Europe. As of 1993, Poland retained the death penalty within their penal code. The punishment could be applied to eight offenses: homicide, high treason, attack on the independence of the state, espionage, terrorist attempts, sabotage, armed robbery, and failure of a soldier to obey an order during combat, as well as three other offenses described in the supplemental laws. These supplementary laws cite genocide and two offenses concerning Polish citizens accepting service in a foreign military organization. According to the Penal Code of 1963, the death penalty cannot be imposed against individuals under the age of 18 or pregnant women. The method utilized by Poland is hanging, unless the offender has committed a military offense, and then the method is shooting.

Over the last 22 years, there have been 204 individuals sentenced to death, and only 2 were not for homicides. The death penalty has not been imposed since 1988, with two exceptions occurring in 1992. Poland has not signed the Second Optional Protocol to the International Covenant on Civil and Political Rights or the European Convention on Human Rights and Fundamental Freedoms.[28] But in 1997, Poland officially abolished the death penalty for all crimes.[29]

Slovenia, a former member of Yugoslavia, no longer retains the death penalty. It too abolished it shortly after the fall of Communism in Eastern Europe. The death penalty was officially abolished in 1989, although Slovenia had been a de facto abolitionist country since 1957 when the last execution was administered. The Czech and Slovak Republics are similar to Slovenia. After the fall of Communism, the Czech Republic, through an amendment to the Criminal Law Act of 1990, abolished the death penalty, substituting life imprisonment as the punishment for serious crimes, predominately homicide. The Slovak Republic also followed suit, two years later on September 1, 1992.[30]

Africa–Ghana, Kenya, Nigeria, and South Africa

The continent of Africa contains fifty-three countries, many of whom have had volatile histories. As of 1991, 4 countries had abolished the death penalty. In the six-year period since 1991, 4 more countries, South Africa included, abolished the punishment. But 2 countries, during this time, reversed their abolition and reinstated the death penalty. As of December 1996, 13 countries were de facto abolitionist, having not carried out an execution in more than ten years. As of January 1997, 30 countries in Africa retained the death penalty. There have been two major reasons for the setbacks to the abolition movement in Africa. First, the economic instability in many of the African countries has resulted in rising crime rates and poverty. Second, profound political instability has plagued many African countries. The persistent argument for retaining the death penalty is that it is a deterrent and public opinion supports it.[31]

Of the four African countries analyzed, South Africa, since 1997, is the only country that has abolished the death penalty for all crimes. Prior to 1997, the death penalty could be imposed by the Supreme Court for seven crimes: murder, treason, robbery, attempted robbery with aggravating circumstances, kidnapping, child-stealing, and rape. The method of execution was typically hanging. The death sentence, though, was not a mandatory sentence. Since 1991, the judges had the right to decide the punishment. Persons under the age of 18 at the time of the crime were exempt from the death sentence.[32]

Individuals who have been sentenced to death have the right to appeal the decision, and if they fail to ask for clemency or utilize their right to appeal, lawyers can take up their appeal for them. Between 1980 and 1989, there were a total of 1,122 executions carried out. Between 1989 and 1992, 442 people were sentenced to death. People were still being sentenced to death until 1995, when the death penalty was abolished for ordinary crimes.[33] The last execution occurred in 1991.[34]

In Ghana, changes have been made regarding the death penalty and capital offenses. Before 1993 and the abolishment of the National Public Tribunal, the tribunal had the jurisdiction to impose death sentences. The use of these tribunals was primarily a way of detaining the opposing political parties and groups by fabricating crimes and allegations against them. Those detained were often not tried or charged because of the possibility they would be executed. But this was not always the case, and the Ghanian system was perverted, and innocent people were executed.[35] The number of people who have been executed over the past five to ten years is unknown. Most offenders that have been executed since 1975 were convicted of felony treason and conspiracy to overthrow the government of Ghana. The method utilized is the firing squad. The age of responsibility is 18.[36]

Kenya also retains the death penalty. The issue of whether to abolish the death penalty was debated in their parliament in 1994, but was ultimately defeated. During that debate, Kiraitu Murungi, a human rights lawyer, stated that the use of the death penalty as the punishment for violent robberies in 1975 has not had any deterrent effect. In fact since 1975, the number of violent robberies has risen.[37] The death penalty is applicable in murder, treason, and violent robberies. The method is hanging. In order for a death sentence to be carried out, the president of the republic must sign off on the execution. The public is not informed of the signing, therefore relatives and friends have no idea when their loved ones have been killed, or even if they have been killed since their sentencing and imprisonment may have occurred some twenty years earlier. The age of criminal responsibility is 18.[38]

Nigeria is slightly different from Ghana and Kenya. While all three countries were former members of the British Empire, Nigeria had the added variable of a large Muslim population. A special panel was established in order to take into account Muslim interests, values, and standards. Muslims live primarily in the north and have established a separate penal code.[39] Treason and armed robbery are the most frequent types of crimes that result in a death sentence.[40] A person convicted of murder, armed robbery, firearms, currency offenses, or treason receives a death sentence. The age of criminal responsibility is 17. The penalty is death by firing squad. The punishment is also done publicly. In November 1992, the punishment for narcotic drug smuggling or possession was changed from death to life imprisonment.[41]

Middle East–Israel, Saudi Arabia, and Iran

Israel, Saudi Arabia, and Iran vary greatly from each other. Each is highly influenced by their religion. The primary religion in each country is different and ultimately molds the individual country's ideology regarding the death penalty.

In Israel, there are two crimes for which a death sentence may be imposed: offenses against humanity and against the Jewish People committed by the Nazis and their abettors; and treason, in wartime. The execution of Adolph Eichmann is the only time the death penalty was imposed since the founding of the state in 1948.[42]

Saudi Arabia has a much more colorful history when it comes to the death penalty. Their criminal justice system is based on the Shari'a, particularly the Hanbali school of Sunni Islam. The Hanbali system of jurisprudence gives prominence to the traditions and sayings of Muhammad. Most Muslim jurists regard this system as especially rigid.[43]

Saudi Arabia has one of the highest execution rates in the world in both numbers and per capita. The types of crimes that are punishable by death include a wide range of offenses, such as apostasy, drug dealing, sodomy, and "witchcraft." Frequently, those found guilty of nonviolent crimes are put to death after a summary trial in which they were not represented by a lawyer and had no opportunity to defend themselves. Executions are by public beheadings for men; women are executed by firing squad or beheading, sometimes in public. Married people who are convicted of an adulterous affair may be executed by stoning to death. Those who have been convicted of serious violent crimes may be crucified. There are also no safeguards to protect those under the age of 18 from being charged, convicted, and ultimately sentenced to death.[44] Anyone who voices a dissenting opinion about the government is likely to be jailed. Women constantly face a risk of being imprisoned. Anyone in a position of influence, especially those among the religious minorities and those who have been deemed to have broken any moral codes, are at risk of imprisonment and conviction.[45]

Secrecy and fear permeate every aspect of the political and state structure of Saudi Arabia. The secrecy extends to the crime and the trial. The offender often finds himself trapped in the judicial system, with no information about his own fate or the ability to contact family, friends, or even a lawyer. The secrecy of the trial also includes the sentence of death. Often the offender has no idea of his sentence until the day of his execution. For those who are in prison and fear they have been sentenced to death, the psychological torment can be unbelievable. Family and friends of those who are incarcerated and fear their loved ones have been given a death sentence also suffer extreme psychological pain.[46]

In 1995, statistics released by the Ministry of Justice stated that there were 457 capital cases pending. Amnesty International recorded that there were 1,163 executions between 1980 and December 1999, but the real number is probably much higher. The scope of the death penalty is so broad that it can be applied to any act the government or the courts deem as "corruption on earth."[47]

Iran is similar to Saudi Arabia, except it is controlled by another faction of Islam. Unfair trials, prisoners of conscience, and persecuted minorities all exist at the hands of an unjust judicial system.[48] By the end of 1999, Iran had executed 165 people. Since 1990, Iran is one of six countries known to have executed child offenders under the age of 18.[49] Like Saudi Arabia, the law is vaguely worded regarding political offenses and those relating to freedom of belief. Unfair trials also occur frequently. Today, an unknown number of people remain under the sentence of death in Iran.[50]

Asia–Pakistan, India, China, and Japan

Pakistan retains the death penalty and imposes it for a large number of offenses. These offenses include murder, felony murder, kidnapping for ransom, hijacking, *zina* (sexual intercourse between unmarried partners) and rape, blasphemy, and drug trafficking. The death penalty is mandatory for *zina*, *zina-bil-jabr* (rape), murder, and blasphemy. Murder is the most common crime that results in the death penalty, at least according to official figures. The method utilized in Pakistan is dependent on the crime. The method for blasphemy and *zina* is stoning to death, although it has never actually been carried out. Hanging is the method used in all other cases. In June 1996, the federal cabinet abolished the death penalty for women, although it has not been certified by the parliament. There was a Child Offender Bill also pending as of 1996 that proposed no person below the age of 16 may be sentenced to death, but these requirements still fall short of the UN Convention on the Rights of the Child. While there is pending legislation, Pakistan is one of the few countries in the world that still executes juveniles.[51]

Pakistani law contains a different ideology than any of the other countries studied thus far. There are two forms of punishment for those who commit murder, homicide, or infliction of injury. Those two options are *qisas* (equal punishment for the crime committed) or *diyat* (compensation payable to the victim or the heirs of the victim). The concept of *qisas* is defined as "punishment by causing similar hurt at the same part of the body of the convict as he has caused to the victim or by causing his death if he has committed *qatl-i-amd* (intentional killing), in exercise of the right of the victim or the *wali* (heir of the victim or the provincial government if there is no heir)." The victim's family also has the ability to pardon the offender and save him from the death penalty.[52]

Sexual crimes are punishable by stoning to death if the individual is *muhsan* (an adult Muslim who is not insane and has had unlawful sexual intercourse) or 100 lashes if the individual convicted is not *muhsan*. If the convict is being stoned, he may also be shot dead, at which time the execution stops. Blasphemy is also a crime that results in the death penalty if the name of the Prophet Muhammad is defamed. Religious offenses against Islam, particularly, singles out the religious minorities such as Christians and Ahmadis, as well as members of the Sunni majority.[53]

Trials sentencing death to individuals do not appear to meet even the minimum standards established in the international standards. The sentence of death is also applied arbitrarily; those who are poor are more likely to be executed than those who are rich. The Qisas and Diyat Ordinance allows for those who have money to buy their freedom.[54]

The death penalty is considered a method of deterrence in Pakistan, but like in so many other countries that continue to use the death penalty, there are no statistics that support this belief. Public executions are conducted, even if the observers are only other prisoners.[55] In 1998, 3,231 people were reported to be on death row in Pakistan, one of the largest death row populations in the world. That same year, 433 people were sentenced to death, and 21 were executed. According to the annual report of the nongovernmental Human Rights Commission of Pakistan, there were 3,480 children in prison, 49 under sentence of death. The only country with more children on death row was the

United States, where at the end of 1998, 73 juveniles were living on death row. In Pakistan, the definition of a child, according to the Hadood laws of 1979, is someone who has not reached puberty. The Hadood laws provide fixed sentences, but in practice they have never been applied to a child. Pakistan ratified the UN Convention on the Rights of the Child in 1990, which states that a child under the age of 18 cannot be sentenced to death. But Pakistan has continued to place children on death row and execute them at intervals.[56]

India also continues to retain the death penalty, although the actual execution of individuals is rare. In 1993, there were only three hangings, and in 1994, there were two. The death penalty is usually reserved for crimes such as political assassinations and multiple murders. The court system is much more like the Anglo-American system. Constitutional guarantees protect the accused, as do provisions defined in the 1973 Penal Code. The court system is also relatively independent, therefore it is less likely to be as corrupt as the court systems in other countries.[57] But those who are executed tend to be poor and illiterate. Statistics on the death penalty are still unavailable.[58]

China has taken the idea of deterrence and crime prevention to a new level and has implemented the death penalty as the method for controlling its crime rate. The number of offenses punishable by death in China has increased from 21 in 1980 to 68, the highest figure in any country. Many of these crimes are nonviolent. Every year there are more people executed in China then there are in the rest of the world put together. Amnesty International reported there were 3,610 death sentences and 2,535 executions in 1995.[59]

Defendants can be tried without warning, and therefore are not always given the time or option to contact a lawyer. Executions are carried out as quickly as the trial, as soon as the higher court has signed off on the judgment. The swiftness of the judicial system has caused some people to be executed days after their alleged crime. The method is usually by firing squad. Repeat offenders, escaped prisoners, and members of gangs may be eligible for the death penalty because of their past actions, not because they have committed a crime in the present.[60]

Typically, the death penalty is applied to crimes such as murder, rape, and serious property crimes. Juveniles can not be punished by death if they were under the age of 18 at the time of the crime, nor can women who are pregnant at the time of adjudication. But if the crime is particularly heinous, juveniles between the ages of 16 and 18 may receive a death sentence, although they will not be executed until after they turn 18. Individuals who are sentenced to death are given a two-year suspension of execution if their immediate execution is not necessary. During these two years, the offender, through repenting and meritorious service, may have their sentence reduced to a fixed imprisonment of between 15 and 20 years.[61]

Japan also continues to utilize the death penalty for certain crimes. Specifically there are 14 crimes that are punishable by death, but in practice only murder and robbery that results in the death of an individual results in a death sentence. The method of execution is hanging. In recent years, the death penalty has been a controversial subject, and there has been a movement toward its abolition.[62] But according to polls, public opinion within Japan continues to support the use of the death penalty.[63]

Executions in Japan have gradually decreased over the last decade. In the three years between 1990 and 1993, there were no executions. Currently there are many individuals awaiting their execution, but less and less are actually being executed. This could be a result of the trend toward abolishment that has been prompted by the United Nations and a series of cases that have shown the injustices which have occurred in recent years.[64]

Southeast Asia–Malaysia, Singapore, and Vietnam

The trend in Southeast Asia has been toward the abolition of the death penalty. But many of the countries still retain it, although they may not carry out any executions.

Malaysia both retains the death penalty and continues to carry out executions. The death penalty is mandatory for trafficking in specific drugs, murder, and certain firearm offenses. Over the years, the executions have declined, but between 1970 and March 1996, there were 349 executions, according to government statistics. Between 1990 and March 1996, 139 executions were carried out, mostly for drug trafficking. As of July 1996, 245 people remained under the sentence of death. The method of execution is hanging.[65]

Singapore also continues to utilize the death penalty. It has discretionary sentences of death for seven different offenses and a mandatory death sentence for murder, treason, certain firearm offenses, and trafficking of certain drugs. While a convict may appeal the decision, clemency is rarely granted. The number of prisoners awaiting their death is unknown, although Amnesty International is aware that at least 34 death sentences were passed in 1995 and at least 16 in the beginning of 1996. These figures, though, are most likely less than the actual figures. The same can be said for the number of executions that have occurred. Amnesty International is aware of 50 executions in 1995 and at least 32 in the early months of 1996. According to the Ministry of Information in Singapore, 76 people were executed in 1994, although that number is probably much less than the actual figure. The method of execution is hanging.[66]

Most executions result from conviction of drug-related offenses. Between 1994 and early 1996, over 150 people were put to death due to drug offenses.

Foreigners are not exempt from the harsh penalties in Singapore and are included in their statistics. The Arms Offenses Act was amended to include mandatory death sentences for both those who use a firearm in the commission of a crime, as well as any accomplices, even if no deaths resulted from the crime. Despite these crackdowns on drug and firearm offenses, there does not appear to be any effect on the drug addiction within Singapore. Many addicts who are charged with trafficking because of the amount of drugs within their possession are executed, while the true traffickers continue to evade punishment.[67]

Vietnam, still uses the death penalty, but it does not have any mandatory sentence restrictions. The death penalty is applicable to a wide range of offenses, but the punishment of death is optional. The crimes range from rape and murder to espionage and terrorism. Drug manufacturing and trafficking was made a capital offense in December 1992. An individual has the right to appeal the decision. The numbers reported by the People's Supreme Court for 1996 were that in the first nine months, 81 people were sentenced to death; in 1995, 104 were sentenced. There are no official statistics for the number of people executed. The method is by firing squad.[68]

The numbers of executions are not only kept secret from outside countries, but executions are not publicized within the country either. There is also a fear that individuals have not received adequate trials and innocent people have been sentenced, and possibly executed.[69]

The belief that the death penalty is a deterrent, that crime rates will go down, and the dependency on public opinion to decide what is right has led many countries to continue to sentence men, women, and children to death. The United States continues to be the only Western democratic nation to utilize the penalty for ordinary crimes and with great frequency.

For more data on the methods of execution, the number of executions worldwide from 1980 to 1999, an account of the countries who have executed child offenders in the 1990s, and the number of abolitionist countries each year from 1981 through 1991, see tables A.6 through A.9 in the appendix.

Notes

1. Amnesty International: Facts and Figures on the Death Penalty.
2. Ibid.
3. Ibid.
4. Ibid.
5. Deathpenaltyinfo.org., 2.
6. NACDL Death Penalty Defense, 1–2.

7. Ibid., 2.

8. World Factbook of Criminal Justice Systems.

9. Amnesty International Report—22/013/1999.

10. Ibid.

11. Library of Congress Country Studies–Belize: Criminal Justice System.

12. Ibid., Colombia: The Penal System.

13. Amnesty International USA Annual Report 1999–Colombia.

14. Library of Congress Country Studies–Colombia: Crime and Political Violence.

15. Death Penalty: When Life Generates Death (Legally).

16. Alaska Justice Forum, 5.

17. World Factbook of Criminal Justice Systems–Germany.

18. Alaska Justice Forum, 5.

19. World Factbook of Criminal Justice Systems–Italy.

20. Ibid., France.

21. Ibid., Russia.

22. Amnesty International: Facts and Figures on the Death Penalty.

23. Death Penalty March 2000 News.

24. World Factbook of Criminal Justice Systems–Ukraine.

25. Amnesty International Report–EUR 57/10/96, 6–7.

26. Ibid., 8.

27. Ibid., 9.

28. World Factbook of Criminal Justice Systems—Poland.

29. Alaska Justice Forum, 5.

30. World Factbook of Criminal Justice Systems—Slovenia, Czech Republic, and Slovak Republic.

31. Amnesty International Report–AFR 01/03/97, 2–3.

32. World Factbook of Criminal Justice System–South Africa.

33. Ibid.

34. Alaska Justice Forum, 5.

35. Amnesty International Report—AFR 01/03/97.

36. World Factbook of Criminal Justice Systems–Ghana.

37. Amnesty International Report—AFR 01/03/97.

38. World Factbook of Criminal Justice Systems–Kenya.

39. Ibid., Nigeria.

40. Amnesty International Report—AFR 01/03/97, 6.

41. World Factbook of Criminal Justice Systems–Nigeria.

42. Ibid., Israel.

43. Library of Congress Country Studies–Saudi Arabia: Criminal Justice System.

44. Amnesty International–MDE 23/01/00.

45. Amnesty International–MDE 23/009/2000.

46. Amnesty International–MDE 23/001/2000.

47. Ibid.

48. Amnesty International Report 1999–Iran.

49. Amnesty International: Facts and Figures on the Death Penalty.

50. Amnesty International Report 1999–Iran.
51. Amnesty International Report–ASA 33/10/96–Pakistan.
52. Ibid.
53. Ibid.
54. Ibid.
55. Ibid.
56. Amnesty International Report—ASA 33/10/96, AI index.
57. Library of Congress Country Studies–India: Criminal Law and Procedure.
58. Amnesty International Report—ASA 20/031/1999, AI index.
59. Amnesty International: *People's Republic of China* (1997).
60. Ibid., China.
61. World Factbook of Criminal Justice Systems–China.
62. Ibid., Japan.
63. http://www.sfc.keio.ac.jp/~jay/1997/Death/pubop2.htm
64. Ibid.
65. Amnesty International Report–ASA 03/01/97–Malaysia
66. Ibid., Singapore.
67. Ibid., Singapore.
68. Ibid., Vietnam.
69. Ibid., Vietnam.

3

Public Opinion on the Death Penalty

A S WE SHOW IN THE PARAGRAPHS that follow, many of the citizens in countries that have abolished the death penalty favor its use. And in countries that have retained the death penalty, it continues to receive public support. Before we report the public's opinions about retaining or abolishing the death penalty, about the types of crimes for which it should be invoked, and about its effectiveness as a deterrent, a few comments about the public opinion data might be useful.

Writing in 1973 in *Public Opinion in America: 1936–1970*, I quoted first from James Bryce, who said in 1962 that "public opinion is the aggregate of views people [men] hold regarding matters that affect or interest the community." I then stated that "public opinion is the verbal response that a representative sample of adults in the United States make to various questions about national policy that are put to them by experts who tell us that these are the important issues of the day." It is with these definitions in mind that we examine public opinion about the death penalty.

Public attitudes concerning the death penalty in the United States can be traced back more than 60 years to 1936, when the public was first asked: Are you in favor of the death penalty for murder? Table 3.1 describes the public responses from 1936 to 1996.

Except for a few select years (1957, 1965, 1966, and 1971) between 1957 and 1971, a majority of the American public consistently stated that they favored the death penalty for persons convicted of murder. They did so between 1972 and 1977 when the death penalty had been outlawed in every jurisdiction in the United States, and they continued to do so by majorities of over 60 percent since it was reinstated. In the decade from 1986 to 1996, between 70 and

Table 3.1
Do You Favor or Oppose the Death Penalty

Capital Punishment–Do you favor or oppose the death penalty for someone convicted of murder?

	Favor	Oppose	DK
1936[a]	62	33	5
1936[a]	59	38	3
1937[a]	61	33	7
1953[b,c]	68	26	6
1956[b]	53	34	13
1957[b]	47	34	18
1960[b]	53	36	11
1965[b]	45	43	12
1966[b]	42	47	11
1967[b]	54	38	8
1969[b]	51	40	9
1971[b]	48	41	11
1972[b]	51	41	8
1972[b]	60	30	10
1972[b]	53	39	8
1973[b]	60	35	5
1974	63	32	5
1975	60	33	7
1976	66	30	5
1976[b]	67	27	7
1977	67	26	6
1978	62	26	11
1978	66	28	6
1979	65	27	8
1980	67	27	6
1981[b]	66	25	9
1982	74	21	6
1982	71	20	9
1983	73	22	5
1984	70	24	6
1985	76	19	5
1985[b]	72	20	8
1985[b]	75	17	8
1986	71	23	5
1987	70	24	6
1988	71	22	7
1989	74		
1990	75		
1991	72		
1993	72		
1994	75		
1996	72		

[a] Are you in favor of the death penalty for murder?
[b] Are you in favor of the death penalty for persons convicted of murder?
[c] "Yes" includes qualified yes; "no" includes qualified no.

75 percent of the American public stated their support for the death penalty. But when the choice is between life without parole and the death penalty, support for the death penalty drops sharply. For example, in 1998 a New York poll found that 44 percent supported life without parole as opposed to 38 percent who supported the death penalty. A *Washington Post*–ABC News national poll conducted in April 2001 found that when asked: Do you favor or oppose the death penalty for persons convicted of murder, 63 percent favored and 28 percent opposed the death penalty. When asked: Which punishment do you prefer for people convicted of murder, the death penalty or life in prison with no chance of parole, the percent favoring the death penalty dropped to 46. Forty-five percent favored life in prison.

Women and African Americans have been consistently less supportive of the death penalty than men and Caucasians; but as shown in percentages below, the differences have gotten smaller between the 1970s and the 1990s.

Table 3.2
Race and Gender Differences about the Death Penalty (in Percent)

	Gender	Race
1970s	+12.7	+29.5
1980s	+10.5	+29.9
1990s	+9.9	+24.7
2001	+14.0	

The male edge in support of the death penalty dropped from 13 percentage points to 10 percentage points from the 1970s to the 1990s, but then increased to 14 percentage points in 2001. The pro-death penalty support led by whites fell from 30 percentage points in the 1970s and 1980s to 25 percentage points in the 1990s.

The responses of the American public are generally supportive of the government policy vis à vis the death penalty. But as we look at the responses shown below, we see that in many of the countries that have abolished the death penalty, the public also continues to favor it. Look, for example, at Canada, Australia, and Great Britain.

Table 3.3
Percent Favoring the Death Penalty

Canada		Australia	
1987	73	1982	55
1995	69		
Great Britain			
1966	76	1984	78
1975	82	1994	

Shown below are other countries in which the public continues to support the death penalty after it was outlawed.

Table 3.4
Percent Favoring the Death Penalty

South Africa		France	
1994	70	1991	59
1995	77		
1996	71		

Among the countries that continue to use the death penalty, the public indicates that they support the policy. Look first, for example, at Eastern Europe.

Table 3.5
Percent Favoring the Death Penalty

Russia	
1997	70
Ukraine	
1995	95
Lithuania	
1993	82
1996	75
Czechoslovakia	
1994	76
1995	67
Bulgaria	
1996	82
Poland	
1996	60

Between 60 and 95 percent of the public in the former Soviet Bloc support retention of the death penalty.

In Asia, in 1994, 74 percent of the Japanese public indicated its support for retention of the death penalty, as opposed to 71 percent in 1967. A national poll conducted in 1999 reported that 80 percent expressed approval for Japan's continued use of the death penalty. Eight percent favored abolition of the death penalty.

Germany provides a rare example of an opposite trend. Shortly after the end of the Second World War, 74 percent of the West German public supported the death penalty, and a majority continued to do so until 1967. But from the 1970s until 1980, there was a sharp decline in support, such that in 1980, 26 percent favored the death penalty, 55 percent opposed it, and 19 percent were undecided. The Federal Republic of Germany abolished the death penalty in 1949, and the German Democratic Republic abolished it in 1987.

In the 1990s, the public in four countries (Canada, Japan, Czechoslovakia, and South Africa) were asked why they supported the death penalty. In all, the major reason was the same: they believed it helped to deter and reduce crime, especially murder. In South Africa, 77 percent of the public want the death penalty restored because of soaring crime rates. They believe the death penalty would serve as a deterrent.

We noted that in the United States, men were more likely than women to support the death penalty. In other countries where the responses were broken by gender, the same pattern prevailed. Men in Japan, Canada, and Australia were more supportive of the death penalty than women.

Table 3.6
Percent Favoring the Death Penalty

	Men	Women
Canada	41	32
Australia	74	70
Japan	74	67

In those same countries, the more educated the respondents the more opposed they are to the death penalty.

While it may not be surprising that in November 1995, 91 percent of white South Africans supported the death penalty, the fact that 69 percent of the black population, 85 percent of the coloreds, and 92 percent of the Indians also supported it is surprising. In Nigeria, 47 percent supported the death penalty in 1990.

In the recent Millennium study conducted by Gallup International, the percentages of those in favor of the death penalty by geographic location were analyzed. Surprisingly, Latin America and Western Europe were the only geographic areas that had a higher percentage of people who were against the death penalty.

Chapter 3

Table 3.7
Percents In Favor and Opposed to the Death Penalty (2000)

	Favor	Oppose
Total	52	39
North America	66	27
Southeast Asia	63	21
Eastern Europe	60	29
Africa	54	43
Latin America	37	55
Western Europe	34	60

In sum, the poll data show widespread support for either retaining or restoring the death penalty for murder and, in some countries, for other violent acts. They also show that men are more likely to support the death penalty than women.

4

Deterrence

IN JANUARY OF 2000, at her weekly Justice Department news briefing, then U.S. Attorney General Janet Reno said, "I have inquired for most of my adult life about studies that might show the death penalty is a deterrent. And I have not seen any research that would substantiate that point." The absence of such data was documented most convincingly by Roger Hood in his 1996 book *The Death Penalty: A Worldwide Perspective.* Hood thoroughly reviewed the research to date on the potential deterrent effect of the death penalty and concluded that

> Research has failed to provide scientific proof that executions have a greater deterrent effect than life imprisonment and such proof is unlikely to be forthcoming. The evidence as a whole still gives no positive support to the deterrent hypothesis.[1]

Hood prefaced his review of the deterrence argument by noting that, despite the low probability of actually being executed for a capital homicide, many retentionist countries claim deterrence as their primary justification for executions. Both China and Saudi Arabia, for example, cite the death penalty as a principle factor in their reduced crime rates.[2] Hood went on to identify four categories of deterrence theory analysis: examination of murder rates before and after the abolition or reintroduction of the death penalty; comparison of murder rates between jurisdictions that differ in their use of the death penalty; examination of crime rates in one location before and after a publicized execution; and studies that employ statistical theory and econometric analysis.[3]

Examining first the impact of abolition or reintroduction of capital punishment, Hood found "persuasive *a priori* evidence that countries need not fear sudden and serious changes in the curve of crime if they reduce their reliance on the death penalty."[4] For example, both Canada and Australia experienced a decrease and no change in homicide rates, respectively, after abolishing the death penalty, and both the United States and Nigeria experienced increases in crime rates after the introduction and reintroduction of the death penalty.[5] In countries like the United Kingdom, which experienced an increase in murder rates after abolishing capital punishment, "Homicide rates lagged a long way behind increases in violent offenses in general."[6]

In July 2000, the National Coalition to Abolish the Death Penalty (NCADP) reported that the five countries with the highest homicide rates that do not impose the death penalty average 21.6 murders per 100,000 people, whereas the five countries with the highest homicide rates that do impose the death penalty average 41.6 murders per 100,000 people. In that same report, the NCADP states that the average murder rate per 100,000 people in U.S. states with capital punishment is about 8 percent, while it is 4.4 percent in abolitionist states. Hood states that between 1980 and 1985, the murder rate fell by 21 percent in Florida and by 25 percent in Georgia, two states that employ the death penalty. During that same time period, the murder rate in New York, a state without the death penalty, also decreased by 26 percent.[7] Hood acknowledges that many of the comparative studies have methodological weaknesses, but he argues that "the fact that the results all point in the same direction is particularly significant."[8]

Table 4.1
Comparison of Abolition and Capital Punishment States

Year	Abolition States	Capital Punishment States
	Maine Rhode Island Michigan Kansas Minnesota	New Hampshire Connecticut Ohio Missouri Indiana
1914	39.4	56.0
1915	37.2	52.4
1916	39.8	54.4
1917	41.0	69.6
1918	31.0	54.8
1919	38.2	55.6
1920	33.0	50.4
1921	44.0	58.8
Average	37.9	56.5

But going back much earlier in *Story of Punishment: A Record of Man's Inhumanity*, Harry Elmer Barnes compared homicide rates for states that had abolished capital punishment against states that retained it, from 1911 through 1921.

Studies that have evaluated the short-term impacts of publicized executions on homicide rates have found some evidence for the "brutalization effect." Not only did the executions not appear to deter homicides, they may have encouraged them by lowering inhibitions against killing. Again, substantial methodological concerns with these short-term studies weaken the brutalization argument. "None the less," Hood points out, "they too provide no evidence that executions depress levels of homicide."[9]

The most recent category of studies examined by Hood is cross-sectional and time-series studies that use multiple regression to try and isolate the variable or variables that influence murder rates. It is this category of analysis that has produced the most convincing evidence for the deterrent effect of capital punishment. The most well-known study of this type was an analysis of capital punishment and murder rates in the United States from 1935 to 1969, conducted by Isaac Ehrlich. Ehrlich concluded that, essentially, each execution results in seven or eight fewer murders. More recently, a study by Stephen Layson replicated Ehrlich's design and found what Hood describes as "undoubtedly the strongest and most uncompromisingly presented evidence of a possible deterrent effect of the death penalty."[10]

In 1983, Archer, Gartner, and Bettel reported the results of an examination of the Comparative Crime Data File (CCDF) using 14 cases to test whether abolition of the death penalty results in an increase or decrease in homicide rates between the year prior to abolition, the year after abolition, and five years after abolition.[11] The data in table 4.2 compare homicide rates between the year prior to abolition and the year after abolition.

The data show little change. In 8 of the 14 cases (57 percent), there was a decrease in the homicide rates following abolition, and in five (36 percent) countries, there was an increase. New Zealand is not included because the 100 percent increase is based on a change from 1 to 2 cases.

The data in table 4.3 compare longer intervals.

Again we see little evidence that the death penalty has a deterrent effect. Half of the jurisdictions for which there is a five-year interlude from the time the death penalty had been abolished show an increase in homicide rates, and the other half show a decrease in homicide rates. Where longer intervals are available, only 5 of the 14 jurisdictions show increases in homicide rates after the death penalty had been abolished. Eight show decreases in the jurisdictions' homicide rates.

The data in the CCDF also allow comparison of crimes other than homicide and the abolition of the death penalty. Is there an increase or decrease in crime rates for robbing, rape, theft, etc., as a result of the abolition of the death

Table 4.2
Homicide Rate Levels before and after Abolition: One Year Comparisons

Jurisdiction	Date of Abolition	Offense Indicator*	One Year Pre-Abolition Homicide Rate	One Year Post-Aboliton Homicide Rate	% Change
Austria	1968	e	.72	.71	−1
England and Wales	1965	a	.36	.35	−3
Finland	1949	a	1.05	.72	−31
Helsinki	1949	a	1.95	1.90	−3
Israel	1954	a	4.00	1.72	−57
Italy	1890	a	13.30	12.94	−3
Sweden	1921	b	.43	.15	−65
Switzerland	1942	d	45.25	35.65	−21
Vienna	1968	e	.93	.93	0
Canada	1967	a	1.10	1.52	38
Denmark	1930	c	33.89	35.68	5
Netherlands Antilles	1957	a	13.19	20.32	54
New Zealand	1961	b	.04	.08	100**
Norway	1905	b	.35	.39	11

*Key to Offense Indicators:
  a = homicide offenses known
  b = murder, manslaughter, or homicide convictions
  c = violent offenses known
  d = violent-offense convictions
  e = criminal statistics
**Because of an extremely low base rate, this 100% increase reflects a change from 1 to 2 cases.

penalty after one year, five years, or whatever the passing possible years are? These results are reported in table 4.4.

Note that for all three time periods, the non-capital offense rates show increases that are larger than the changes reported for homicide rates. Clearly, these results contradict the hypotheses of offense deterrence. The data in all three tables that describe the experience of 14 countries over different time periods do not support the hypothesis that the death penalty is an effective deterrent for homicide. Its abolition did not lead to an increase in the number of murders committed.

For every statistically sophisticated study that has found evidence of a deterrent effect, more have contested and even discredited the work of Ehrlich and his peers. Studies by Bowers and Pierce; Passell, Black and Orsagh; and Bailey all used similar or even identical methods and found no consistent re-

Table 4.3
Homicide Rate Changes before and after Abolition: Longer Trends

Jurisdiction	One Year	Five Year Means[a]	Maximum Possible Comparison[b]	Years before Abolition/ Years After
Austria	−1%	32%	9%	(15/5)
Canada	38	63	67	(5/6)
Denmark	5	—	4	(9/2)
England and Wales	−3	18	27	(14/7)
Finland	−31	−40	−59	(22/18)
Helsinki	−3	−27	−57	(5/16)
Israel	−57	−53	−65	(10/24)
Italy	−3	−5	−30	
Netherlands Antilles	54	—	−4	(2/13)
New Zealand	100	117	0	(10/11)
Norway	11	—	−24	(2/35)
Sweden	−65	—	−63	(1/28)
Switzerland	−21	−36	−49	(13/28)
Vienna	0	94	85	(15/5)

a = Comparison of mean offense levels for five-year periods before and after abolition
b = Comparison of mean offense levels for maximum-length periods before and after abolition.

lationship between executions and murder rates. Likewise, Brian Forst conducted a combined cross-sectional and time-series approach to study 32 states from 1960 to 1970. Forst included in his multiple regression model a number of social, demographic, and punishment variables. He found no evidence that "those states in which the actual use of capital punishment ceased during the 1960s experienced [any] greater increase in the murder rate than those states that did not use capital punishment in the first place."[12] Altogether, these categories of studies have produced strikingly conflicting results and evidence for both deterrence and brutalization effects.

Since Hood's comprehensive review of the data in 1996, additional studies have been published that echo his findings. For example, a study of death sentences, executions, and the murder rate in Texas between 1984 and 1997 found no evidence of a deterrence effect. The study concluded that the number of executions was unrelated to state murder and felony rates.[13] A similar study of executions and various types of murder in Oklahoma between 1989 and 1991 found no evidence of a deterrent effect. In fact, the study reported a significant increase in stranger killings after Oklahoma resumed executions after a 25-year moratorium.[14] In 1997, the Bureau of Justice Statistics reported that

Table 4.4
Comparison of Homicide Levels before and after Abolition
Using Other Offenses as Control Variables (one year)

Jurisdiction	One Year					
	Homicide	M[b]	R	A	Ro	T
Austria[c]	−1%	+24	+12	−2	−9	+17
Canada	+38	+107	+32	+20	+42	—
Denmark	+5	—	0	+5	—	+8
England	−3	+57	+23	+13	+44	+9
Finland	−31	−27	+95	−10	−46	−43
Israel	−57	—	—	+40	−55	−6
Italy	−3	—	—	−10	+31	+4
Neth. Antilles	+54	—	−50	—	+51	+13
New Zealand	+100	—	+11	+27	−43	−4
Norway	+11	—	+36	−13	—	−10
Sweden	−65	—	−58	−33	−36	—
Switzerland	−21	—	+21	−21	+	+7
Helsinki	−3	−35	+1	+3	−52	−42
Vienna	0	+30	+32	−2	−11	+22
Median	−2%	+27	+12	−2	−11	+6

Comparison of Homicide Levels before and after Abolition
Using Other Offenses as Control Variables (five years)

Jurisdiction	Five Years					
	Homicide	M[b]	R	A	Ro	T
Austria	+32%	+57	+5	+8	+44	+55
Canada	+63	+11	+57	+76	+73	—
Denmark	—	—	—	—	—	—
England	+18	+58	+56	+73	+102	+36
Finland	−40	−44	+28	—	−80	−70
Israel	−53	—	—	—	−75	−8
Italy	−5	—	—	—	+32	—
Neth. Antilles	—	—	—	—	—	—
New Zealand	+117	—	+16	+46	−46	+7
Norway	—	—	—	—	—	—
Sweden	—	—	—	—	—	—
Switzerland	+36	—	—	−36	—	−3
Helsinki	−27	−42	+23	—	−86	+79
Vienna	+94	+100	+6	+20	+49	+53
Median	7%	34	23	33	32	22

Comparison of Homicide Levels Before and After Abolition Using Other Offenses as Control Variables (maximum years)

Jurisdiction	Max. Years Possible[a]					
	Homicide	M[b]	R	A	Ro	T
Austria	+9%	+42	−3	+6	+72	+109
Canada	+67	+21	+68	+79	+78	—
Denmark	+4	—	+25	—	—	+34
England	+27	+30	+86	+196	+248	—
Finland	−59	−63	+102	—	−47	−9
Israel	−65	—	—	—	−74	+60
Italy	−30	—	—	—	+35	—
Neth. Antilles	−4	—	−20	—	+87	+18
New Zealand	0	—	—	—	−12	+46
Norway	−24	—	+100	−7	—	+10
Sweden	−63	—	+123	−3	+19	—
Switzerland	−46	—	—	—	—	−15
Helsinki	−57	−55	+73	—	−71	−43
Vienna	+85	+138	−3	+33	+100	+145
Median	−14%	+26	+71	+20	+35	+26

[a]For the number of years included in this comparison, see table 4.3.
[b]Crime types: M (manslaughter), R (rape), A (assault), Ro (robbery), T (theft).
[c]Indicator Type and Year of Abolition are given in table 4.2.

the south repeatedly has the highest murder rate of any region in the United States and, as a region, accounts for 80 percent of all executions. In contrast, the northeast region, which consists of less than 1 percent of all executions, has the lowest regional murder rate.

As Hood noted earlier, most of the death penalty research continues to be done within the United States. A rare exception was a 1997 study of executions and murder and violent crime rates in 293 countries. The authors matched countries by historical, demographic, and economic variables. The pairs shared contiguous borders but differed regarding the use of capital punishment. No support for the deterrence effect was found, even at the county level, and the authors found higher violent crime rates in death penalty countries.[15]

Hood's prediction, that evidence of the deterrent effect of capital punishment would not be forthcoming, has certainly remained true in the five years since the publication of his book. In sum,

with the lonely exception of Ehrlich, whose work generally has been seriously questioned if not totally discredited, death penalty researchers have found virtually no support for the argument that the level use of capital punishments influences US murder rates.[16]

Notes

1. Roger Hood, *The Death Penalty: A Worldwide Perspective* (Clarendon Press, 1996), 238.

2. Ibid., 180–81.

3. Ibid., 186–87.

4. Ibid., 187.

5. Ibid., 187–89.

6. Ibid., 189.

7. Ibid.

8. Ibid., 237.

9. Ibid.

10. Ibid., 200.

11. "Homicide and the Death Penalty," *Journal of Criminal Law and Criminology* 74 no. 3, 1983: 991–1013.

12. Brian Forst, "Capital Punishment and Deterrence: Conflicting Evidence," *Journal of Criminal Law and Criminology* 74, fall 1983.

13. John Sorenson, Robert Wrinkle, Victoria Brewer, and James Marquet, "Capital Punishment and Deterrence: Examining the Effect of Execution on Murder in Texas." *Crime and Delinquency* 45, 1999: 481–93.

14. William Bailey, "Deterrence, Brutalization and the Death Penalty: Another Examination of Oklahoma's Return to Capital Punishment," *Criminology.* 36, 1998: 711–33.

15. Keith Harries and Derral Cheatwood, *The Geography of Execution: The Capital Punishment Quagmire in America* (Rowman & Littlefield Publishers, Inc., 1997).

16. William C. Bailey and Ruth D. Peterson, "Murder, Capital Punishment and Deterrence: A Review of the Literature," in *The Death Penalty in America: Current Controversies,* edited by Hugo Adam Bedau (publisher, 1997), 143.

5

Execution of Innocents

"It is better to risk saving a guilty person than to condemn an innocent one."

—Voltaire, *Zadig*, 1747

ONE OF THE PRINCIPLE OBJECTIONS to the death penalty is the possibility, however slight, that an innocent person could be executed. As is the case with other aspects of capital punishment, the problem of executing innocent people has been addressed largely in the context of the United States.

United States

The death penalty has recently come under a great deal of public scrutiny, due to widespread concern regarding the potential execution of innocent people. "For the first time in a generation, the death penalty is in the dock—on the defensive . . . for being too arbitrary and too prone to error."[1] According to the Death Penalty Institute, since 1973, 95 prisoners have been released from death row after evidence of their innocence emerged. As Amnesty International noted, "this is equivalent to one acquittal to every seven executions [and] this number may become much higher if DNA testing is allowed in all death penalty cases."[2]

The increased concern regarding the execution of innocents has been fueled by the dramatic findings of recent studies, mainstream media attention, and developments related to the use of DNA in capital cases. In the November 9, 1998, issue of *U.S. News & World Report*, Joseph Shapiro reported that "for every seven executions, 486 since 1976, one other prisoner on death row has been found innocent." Shapiro goes on to state that in Illinois, from 1976 to 1998, eleven men were executed and nine were exonerated and released from prison. The Appeals Court vacated 35 convictions and sentences.

A study released in June 2000 by Columbia University Law School examined death sentences passed between 1973 and 1995 and found that they were "persistently and systematically fraught with error." In fact, the study reported that courts have found serious errors in 68 percent of the 4,578 cases reviewed.[3] Even more disturbing were the findings of a 1987 study by Bedau and Radelet. The authors concluded that 213 innocent people were executed in the United States between 1905 and 1974, and 22 others came within seven hours of their scheduled execution before being granted reprieves.

The most dramatic illustration of increased concern over executing innocents was the moratorium on executions declared by the governor of Illinois, George Ryan, in January 2000. Since the United States reinstated the death penalty in 1977, 13 death row prisoners in Illinois have been exonerated of the crimes for which they were sentenced to death. Explaining his decision, Ryan stated:

> I cannot support a system which, in its administration, has proven so fraught with error and has come so close to the ultimate nightmare, the state's taking of innocent life. . . . Until I can be sure that everyone sentenced to death in Illinois is truly guilty, until I can be sure with moral certainty that no innocent man or woman is facing lethal injection, no one will meet that fate.

Governor Ryan's decision was likely sparked both by the most recent exoneration of an Illinois death row inmate and by the fiercely critical *Chicago Tribune* series on the death penalty, published at the end of 1999. The *Tribune* conducted its own investigation of 285 Illinois death sentences and found that "capital punishment in Illinois is so riddled with faulty evidence, unscrupulous trial tactics, and legal incompetence that justice has been forsaken."[4] Even then Texas Governor George W. Bush—who oversaw 132 executions during his five-year term—granted his first stay of execution ever in 2000. Although Bush did not doubt the guilt of the inmate, he did acknowledge what *Newsweek* described as "the doubts spreading around the country about the fairness of a system with life-and-death stakes."[5]

The problems that frequently plague death penalty cases are prosecutorial or police misconduct, inadequate defense representation, the use of unreliable witness testimony (including jailhouse informants), and the use of unreliable physical evidence or confessions.[6] For example, the *Tribune* investigation found that 40 percent of the 85 death penalty convictions examined included at least one of the following four problems: defense attorneys that were later suspended or disbarred, the use of jailhouse snitches, unreliable hair compar-isons, or black defendants convicted by all white juries. In 1999, the American Bar Association called for a moratorium on the death penalty stating concerns regarding the lack of competent counsel, restricted access to appellate courts even when new evidence of innocence is present, and racial disparities in the administration of capital punishment.[7]

In their book *Convicted But Innocent: Wrongful Conviction and Public Policy*, authors C. Ronald Huff, Aryee Rattner, and Edward Sagarin state that they believe "that the single most important factor leading to wrong-ful convictions in the United States and England . . . is eyewitness misiden-tification." They noted that race further compounds this problem, due to the difficulty victims have distinguishing members of other races from one another. Table 5.1 reproduces the distribution of types of error in 205 wrongful conviction cases evaluated in their book.

As a forensic science, DNA analysis has a relatively short history, dating back only to the late 1980s.[8] DNA has made the process of identifying offenders much more rigorous and less fraught with error. Through the use of DNA evi-dence, prosecutors are now able to conclusively establish the guilt or innocence of a defendant. In fact, more than 70 inmates have been exonerated by DNA ev-idence since 1982, including 11 on death row.[9] Currently, only Illinois and New

Table 5.1
Distribution of Errors Contributing to Wrongful Conviction from
***Convicted But Innocent* (Huff et al.)**

Type of Error	—	%(relative)	%(adjusted)
Eyewitness misidentification	100	48.8	52.3
Perjury by witness	21	10.2	11.0
Negligence by criminal justice officials	19	9.3	9.9
Pure error (2)	16	7.8	8.4
Coerced confession	16	7.8	8.4
"Frame up" (3)	8	3.9	4.2
Perjury by criminal justice professionals	5	2.4	2.6
Identification by police due to prior criminal record	3	1.5	1.6
Forensic errors (4)	3	1.5	1.6
Other errors (missing data)	14	6.8	
Totals	205	100.0	100.0

York give inmates the right to DNA testing. Further evidence of public concern over the execution of innocents is reflected in a *Newsweek* poll that found that 95 percent of Americans want the right to DNA testing guaranteed, and almost 90 percent support the idea of federal guarantees of DNA testing. Convictions that were reversed using DNA evidence include the case of Kirk Bloodsworth, a Maryland man who was sentenced to death for rape and murder in 1985. Bloodsworth was released after DNA evidence made available in 1993 proved he was not the rapist-killer. DNA evidence also exonerated Rolando Cruz, who was sentenced to death in 1985 for the abduction, rape, and murder of a young girl. He was acquitted in 1995 and the prosecution dropped all charges against his alleged co-defendant, as well.

The tragedy of wrongful convictions has often been brought home to the American public by means of high publicity cases. *Convicted But Innocent* highlighted a few of the dramatic cases that have encouraged distrust of the death penalty process throughout history, including the cases of the Scottsboro Boys, Isidore Zimmerman, and Randall Dale Adams.

The Scottsboro Boys were nine young black men who were convicted by an all-white jury of raping two white women in 1927. Eight of the men were sentenced to death in "a process that was somewhat analogous to an assembly line turning out widgets." All told, the men spent "a total of 104 years of their collective lives in prison for crimes that apparently never occurred." This case involved racism, inadequate defense counsel, due process violations, and false rape allegations.

Isidore Zimmerman was sentenced to death in 1937 for supplying guns that were used in the murder of a police officer. Zimmerman was in prison for 24 years and came within two hours of execution before his sentence was downgraded to life. His conviction was eventually reversed in 1967; it then took him an additional 20 years to be awarded financial compensation. "The case involved perjury by a key witness [perjury that was known to the assistant district attorney], prosecutorial overzealousness, and unethical conduct."

Randall Dale Adams was convicted and sentenced to death for the murder of a Texas policeman in 1976. The murder was actually committed by a young man who served as the chief witness in the trial. Adams was awarded a stay of execution just 72 hours before he was scheduled to die by lethal injection. After over 12 years in prison, Adams was freed. This case involved perjured testimony, and overzealousness and unethical behavior on the part of the prosecutor. Adams' story was eventually documented in the 1998 film *The Thin Blue Line.*

In 1993, the subcommittee on Civil and Constitutional Rights, of the Committee of the Judiciary of the United States Congress, issued a report "assessing the danger of mistaken executions." The report concluded that

Judging by past experience, a substantial number of death row inmates are indeed innocent and there is a high risk that some of them will be executed. The danger is inherent in the punishment itself and the fallibility of human nature. . . . Errors can and have been made repeatedly—poor representation, racial prejudice, prosecutorial misconduct, or simply the presentation of erroneous evidence.

Worldwide

In 1994, the United Nations' Human Rights Committee received reports that over 2,300 persons (including 49 minors) had been extra-judicially, summarily, or arbitrarily executed in 51 different countries. This horrific statistic is difficult to support with additional sources, as there is only a limited amount of information available on the execution of innocent people outside the United States.

Roger Hood, in his book *The Death Penalty: A Worldwide Perspective*, observed that the possibility of executing the innocent increases with the speed of trials and executions, and with the use of military tribunals, which acknowledge fewer rights than do civilian courts. According to Hood:

> There were reports of executions [in China] occurring within six to eight days after arrest for the crime. From Iran, also, there have been reports of summary trials for drug offenders and others, with no defense counsel or right to appeal. Both Ethiopia (in 1974) and Pakistan (in 1987) introduced "speedy trial" courts with their attendant limitations and short periods allowed for appeal (seven days only in Pakistan. . .). At various times—in Bangladesh, India, Indonesia, Nigeria, South Korea, Nepal, Taiwan, Chile, Argentina, and Guatemala (though not recently), trials which resulted in the death penalty were held before military tribunals. . . . In India and Sri Lanka, for example, martial law places the burden of proof on the defendant.

Additional problems include poor legal representation—for example, the UN condemned the very low quality of legal aid in the Caribbean—and insufficient translation for foreign defendants. Poland has been criticized for affording inadequate translation and "there have been some disturbing reports that migrant workers in the Middle East and some other parts of the world have not been provided with adequate interpretation and translation of every stage of the legal process."[10] Amnesty International reported that a number of countries have recently released prisoners sentenced to death, after admitting that they had been wrongfully convicted. These countries include the Philippines, Malaysia, Belize, China, Pakistan, Trinidad and Tobago, Malawi, Turkey, and Japan.

Individual International Cases

Middle East

In Israel, John Demjanjuk was sentenced to death in 1988 after being identified as "Ivan the Terrible," a notorious Nazi death camp guard. His sentence was overturned in 1993 after the supreme court, in a rare exception to traditional practice, examined newly discovered evidence.[11]

Western Europe

In 1950, Timothy Evans was executed in England for a murder that was actually committed by the chief witness against him, a man who was later caught and executed. This case was described in detail by Ludovic Kennedy in his book *Ten Rillington Place*. The case and the book are often credited for the abolition of capital punishment in England.[12]

In 1998, an appeals court in the UK posthumously overturned the conviction of a Somali national, Mahamood Hussein Mattan. Mattan was convicted of murder and executed in 1952 after a trial that was "strongly tainted by racism." The court that overturned the conviction 46 years later determined that "the witnesses at the original trial were unreliable and that the prosecutors had withheld evidence."[13]

Eastern Europe

In 1994, Russia executed serial killer Andrei Chikatilo for the murder of 52 people and admitted that they had previously executed "the wrong man" for one of those murders. Alexander Kravchenko was executed after being wrongfully convicted, due largely to the desire on the part of the police to "stop the killings quickly."[14]

In 1998, the Supreme Court of Uzbekistan posthumously overturned the conviction of Vakhobzhan Usmanov, a former government minister who was convicted of corruption and executed in 1986.

As many as 41 capital convictions were reversed in the Ukraine between 1989 and 1993.[15]

Asia

In 1983, the Supreme Court of Japan acquitted Menda Sakae after he had spent 34 years under sentence of death. Sakae had applied for a retrial six times before his application was accepted.

In 1984, the Supreme Court of Japan acquitted both Taniguchi Shigeyoshi and Saito Yukio. Shigeyoshi had been imprisoned under sentence of death since 1952; Yukio had been imprisoned under sentence of death since 1957.

In 1989, the Supreme Court of Japan acquitted Akahori Masao of charges of rape and murder. Masao had been sentenced to death in 1958 and spent over 30 years of his life in prison awaiting execution. Masao was acquitted after his fourth application for a retrial was accepted; the only evidence against him was the false confession forced from him by abusive police interrogators.

In 1990, the Supreme Court of Japan acquitted Shimohami Norio, who had spent 15 years imprisoned and awaiting execution. According to the court, "the evidence against [Norio] was contradictory . . . and untrustworthy."

Between 1989 and 1993, 41 capital cases were overturned or commuted in Bangladesh (four by the president and the remainder by the supreme court).

Today the main rationale behind continuing the execution of criminals is retribution. It supplies the simplest and most direct argument for the death penalty: execute murderers and other heinous criminals because they deserve it. This ideology, though, has created a system resistant to change. In the United States, once a person has been convicted of a crime, it is almost impossible to get their conviction reversed, particularly on the grounds of the accused's innocence.[16] Once an individual has been convicted, the presumption of innocence is lost forever. In 33 states there are statutes of limitations of six months or less on newly discovered evidence of innocence motions. These statutes have been enacted because prosecutors regard the exoneration of an innocent person as a direct attack against the criminal justice system.[17] The consistent disregard for the continued protection of innocence within the United States' criminal justice system is what has caused the added need for increased availability of DNA testing with less statutes restricting time limits on new evidence. Worldwide, the ability to use DNA and other technological methods in order to prove the guilt or innocence of an individual should be supported and enforced. There is nothing more important than the culpability of a defendant, and the use of DNA analysis is able to do just that when the evidence exists. Nothing should stand in the way of that occurring.

Notes

1. "The Death Penalty on Trial." *Newsweek*, June 4, 2000.
2. Amnesty International, "USA: Increasing Concern over Execution of the Innocent," *Death Penalty News*, June 2000.

3. Ibid.

4. "Death Row Justice Derailed" (first of a five-part series). *Chicago Tribune*, November 14, 1999.

5. "The Death Penalty on Trial," *Newsweek*, June 4, 2000.

6. Amnesty International, "USA: Increasing Concern over Execution of the Innocent."

7. Michael Radelet and Hyo Adam Bedau, "The Execution of the Innocent," *Law and Contemporary Problems* 61, Autumn 1998: 105.

8. Edward Conners, Thomas Lundregan, Neal Miller, and Tom McEwen."Convicted by Juries, Exonerated by Science: Case Studies in the Use of DNA Evidence to Establish Innocence after Trial," U.S. Department of Justice, Office of Justice Programs, June 1996.

9. "The Dentist Takes the Stand," *Newsweek*, August 20, 2001.

10. Hood, *The Death Penalty,* 111.

11. Ibid.

12. Huff et al., *Convicted But Innocent.*

13. Amnesty International.

14. Amnesty International.

15. Hood, *The Death Penalty.*

16. Radelet and Bedau, "The Execution of the Innocent," 105.

17. "The Case for Innocence," *Frontline*, interview with Barry Scheck.

6

Genocide and Democide

THE TERM *GENOCIDE* WAS COINED by Raphael Lemkin, a Polish-Jewish lawyer, in 1944.[1] *Genocide* denotes the attempt to destroy a nation or an ethnic group by depriving them of the ability to live and procreate or by killing them directly. At the International Military Tribunal at Nuremberg, following the end of the Second World War, the Nazi plan to annihilate European Jewry was defined as a crime against humanity.

In December 1948, the United Nations General Assembly adopted the Genocide Convention, which stated that "genocide, whether committed in time of peace or in time of war, is a crime under international law which the parties to the convention undertake to prevent and punish."[2] Parties to the convention were obliged to enact implementing legislation to assure punishment of persons guilty of this crime. As of February 28, 1965, 67 nations had become signatories of the convention, but no action has ever been taken.

Gerald Scully, author of *Murder by the State,* reports that "170 million people and perhaps as many as 360 million have been murdered by their own governments" in the twentieth century.[3] According to Scully, when a state murders some of the general population, it is called *democide*; when it murders minorities, the term is *genocide.*

Helen Fein, author of *Accounting for Genocide*, emphasizes that "genocide also differs from collective violence, deliberate injury or extraordinary punishment inflicted against people just because they are members of a collectivity (religious, ethnic or racial group) in that it is centrally planned and purposeful, and in that its intent is total."[4] Genocide eliminates the group.

The first instance of genocide in the twentieth century was the extermination of the Armenians in Turkey in 1915. Some 1,200,000 Armenians, two-thirds of the Armenian community in the Ottoman Empire in 1914, were annihilated.

The three regimes that hold the record for genocide in the twentieth century are the former Soviet Union, Nazi Germany, and the People's Republic of China. Between 1917 and 1987, the Soviet Union killed 54.7 million people.[5] During the reign of Joseph Stalin from 1929 to 1953, some 42.7 million people were killed in the Soviet Union. Nazi Germany killed 17 million people between 1933 and 1945. The Jews were the major, but not the only, group in Nazi Germany targeted for destruction. The Gypsies were also designated for destruction. Under the reign of Mao Tse-tung in China, 34.4 million people were killed between 1949 and 1976. In the following decade, 874,000 were killed.

Relying on information reported by R. J. Rummel, Scully provides data on government sponsored murder in previous centuries. In the thirteenth century, governments murdered about 32.2 million people, which amounted to about 8.9 percent of the total population, estimated at 360 million. In the fourteenth and fifteenth centuries, the Mongols killed about 30 million people. In the seventeenth century, governments murdered about 25.6 million, representing about 4.7 percent of the population. By the nineteenth century, guns were highly developed and widely dispersed. In that century, 44.4 million people were killed by their governments, and the figure represented 3.7 percent of the world's population. In the twentieth century, 7.3 percent of the world's population were killed.

Table 6.1 below describes the country, the time period, and the number of killings committed by governments (democides and genocides) in the twentieth century.

The Communist regimes were responsible for more than 108 million deaths out of an estimated total of 135 million. The Nazi regime contributed an additional 17 million. Combined Communist and Nazi governments were responsible for 93 percent of the state sponsored murders in the twentieth century.

Table 6.2 lists those countries that practiced democide and genocide in the twentieth century and have retained the death penalty for ordinary crimes today.

The countries listed in table 6.3 practiced democide and genocide earlier in the twentieth century and have since done away with the death penalty.

The twentieth century has been called "The Century of Genocide." There have been more deaths caused by genocide, democide, and mass murders than were taken during every war during the century.

Table 6.1
Twentieth-Century Democide and Genocide[6]

Country	Period	Domestic Democide (thousands)	Genocide (thousands)
Communist			
Afghanistan	1978–87	228	0
Albania	1944–87	100	0
Bulgaria	1944–87	222	0
Burma	1962–87	43	0
Cambodia	1975–79	2,000	541
China	1949–87	35,236	375
Cuba	1959–87	73	0
Czechoslovakia	1948–68	65	0
Ethiopia	1974–87	725	0
Germany (E)	1948–87	70	0
Hungary	1948–87	27	0
Korea (N)	1948–87	1,293	60
Laos	1975–87	56	50
Mongolia	1926–87	100	0
Poland	1948–87	22	0
Romania	1948–87	435	0
USSR	1917–87	54,769	10,000
Vietnam	1945–87	944	0
Yugoslavia	1944–87	987	0
Total		97,395	11,026
Africa			
Algeria	1962–87	50	0
Angola	1957–87	125	0
Burundi	1966–87	150	150
Central Afr. Rep.	1966–79	2	0
Chad	1962–87	10	10
Congo	1959–68	5	0
Eq. Guinea	1968–79	50	0
Guinea	1958–84	3	0
Kenya	1964–87	0.5	0
Liberia	1900–87	10	0
Libya	1968–87	1	0
Mozambique	1975–87	198	0
Nigeria	1966–79	400	15
Rwanda	1962–73	15	15
South Africa	1934–87	6	6

(continued)

Chapter 6

Table 6.1 *(Continued)*
Twentieth-Century Democide and Genocide

Country	Period	Domestic Democide (thousands)	Genocide (thousands)
Africa (continued)			
Sudan	1956–87	627	494
Uganda	1960–87	557	22
Zaire	1960–87	6	0
Zanzibar	1964	8	0
Total		2,223.5	712
Latin America			
Dominican Rep.	1930–61	0	5
El Salvador	1984–87	3	0
Grenada	1983	0.11	0
Guatemala	1956–87	122	0
Haiti	1957–86	3	0
Honduras	1982–87	0.15	0
Mexico	1930–87	2	0
Nicaragua	1937–87	20	1
Argentina	1976–87	20	0
Brazil	1945–85	131	125
Chile	1973–87	10	0
Colombia	1948–87	74	5
Paraguay	1954–87	2.3	2
Peru	1980–87	10	0
Uruguay	1973–84	0.3	0
Total		397.86	138
Asia/Middle East			
Bangladesh	1927–87	15	12
India	1950–87	25	15
Indonesia	1965–87	579	200
Iran	1954–87	71	15
Iraq	1963–87	187	145
Israel	1949–87	0	2
Korea (S)	1948–87	23	0
Pakistan	1958–87	1,503	1,500
Philippines	1972–86	15	0
Sri Lanka	1972–87	4	0
Thailand	1976–87	0.1	0
Yemen (N)	1962–87	2.5	0
Yemen (S)	1967–87	1	0
Total		2,425.6	1,889

Europe			
Cyprus	1977–87	2	2
France	1900–44	13.7	4
Germany	1933–45	762	16,315
Greece	1911–54	4	0
Italy	1922–46	1.25	1
Spain	1939–75	275	0
Turkey	1919–87	705	893
United Kingdom	1900–87	0.13	0
Total		1,763.08	17,215
Total (all categories)		104,205.04	30,980

Table 6.2
**Countries That Have Practiced Democide and Genocide
in the Twentieth Century and Retain the Death Penalty**

As of March 1996	
Afghanistan	Kyrgyzstan
Albania	Lao People's
Algeria	Democratic Republic
Armenia	Latvia
Azerbaijan	Liberia
Bangladesh	Lithuania
Belarus	Mongolia
Bulgaria	Nigeria
Chad	Pakistan
China	Poland
Cuba	Republic of Korea
Democratic People's	(South Korea)
Republic of Korea	Russian Federation
Equatorial Guinea	Sudan
Estonia	Tajikistan
Ethiopia	Thailand
Georgia	Uganda
Grenada	Ukraine
India	Uzbekistan
Indonesia	Vietnam
Iran	Yemen
Iraq	Yugoslavia
Kazakhstan	Zaire
Kenya	

Table 6.3
**Countries That Have Practiced Democide and Genocide in
the Twentieth Century and Have Abolished the Death Penalty**

Europe	Africa
Cyprus	Angola
Czechoslovakia	Burundi
France	Central African Republic
Germany	Congo
Greece	Guinea
Hungary	Mozambique
Italy	South Africa
Romania	Zanzibar
Spain	
Turkey	
United Kingdom	
Central and South America	**Middle East and Asia**
Argentina	Burma
Brazil	Cambodia
Chile	Israel
Colombia	Philippines
El Salvador	Sri Lanka
Guatemala	
Haiti	
Honduras	
Mexico	
Nicaragua	
Paraguay	
Peru	
Uruguay	

United States

The United States is not exempt from the crime of genocide. While it is continually overlooked, the lynching of African Americans during the late nineteenth century into the twentieth century should be included in an analysis of genocide and democide. The definition of *lynching* is "the illegal execution of an accused person by a mob"[7] or an "execution without the due process of law."[8] The term *lynch* originated as a result of the activities of Colonel Charles Lynch. Lynch was a colonel during the Revolutionary War. He also owned a wealthy plantation in Virginia and founded an extralegal court. This "court" took the law into its own hands and did not give the accused the right to a real trial.[9] Lynching was a popular method of maintaining white supremacy within most of the states, especially within the Southern states. It has been estimated that on average, between 1880 and 1920, two African Americans per week were lynched.[10] It was not until the 1850s that lynching took an extremely violent turn. Before 1850, victims were only beaten. After 1850, lynching took on the connotation used today. By 1890, lynch mobs took on another level of brutality, when the crowd began to dismember their black victims and sell the body parts as souvenirs.[11] The most common methods for lynching included hanging and shooting, however there were more brutal methods utilized by the white mobs, such as burning at the stake, maiming, dismemberment, castration, and physical torture.[12]

Although lynchings were directed at the black race as a whole, in some states, whites who openly opposed lynchings were killed as well. Seventy-nine percent of lynchings happened in the South; Mississippi had the highest number with 581 between 1882–1968, followed by Georgia with 531 and Texas with 493.[13] According to the Tuskegee Institute, between 1882 and 1951, 4,730 people were lynched; 3,437 were African American and 1,293 were white. The largest number occurred in 1892, when 230 people were murdered. Men were not the only victims of lynch mobs; between 1882 and 1927, 92 women were victims, 26 African Americans and 16 white. These statistics, though, are based primarily on newspaper articles, and therefore are not completely accurate. In fact, more people were most likely killed at the hands of lynch mobs during these times. Many of these people were also innocent of any crime. A study done by Arthur Raper of nearly 100 cases convinced him that approximately one-third of the victims were falsely accused. Occasionally, the mob was even mistaken about the identity of their victim.[14]

With the rise in lynchings in the South due in part to the emancipation following the Civil War and the establishment of the Ku Klux Klan in 1867,[15] an antilynching movement took hold. Its leading voice was Ida B. Wells-Barnett, an African American who in the early 1890s published many pamphlets detailing the horrors of lynching. Rape of a white woman was the leading reason behind many of the lynchings. Wells-Barnett in her pamphlets claimed that many of these encounters were consensual interracial relationships. Because of her claims, she was driven out of her hometown of Memphis, Tennessee, on the threat of being lynched.[16]

The establishment of the National Association for the Advancement of Colored People (NAACP) in 1909, of which Ida B. Wells-Barnett was a founding member, was also highly effective in awakening the nation to the urgency of putting an end to lynching.[17] But lynching was more an expression of white fear of black social and economic advancement than of any crime. Lynchings occurred predominately in smaller towns and rural communities in the South where people were poor and mostly illiterate, and where there was a noticeable lack of wholesome community activities. A lynching became the local community affair. The fundamental cause of most lynches, however, stemmed from the basis of racism and discrimination.[18]

After 1892, a decline in the number of lynching occurred. The exact reason for this decline has never been fully explained. There have been many speculations, for example, the growing distaste of lynchings by the Southern elite. Others mention the urbanization of African Americans in the South during the 1930s and 1940s. There was also the establishment of police systems that were willing to oppose lynch mobs, and the National Guard was frequently called in to stop lynchings. These things coupled together probably played integral parts in the decline of lynchings throughout the country, but specifically within the South.[19]

In 1921, the NAACP sponsored antilynching legislation such as the Dyer Anti-Lynching Bill and numerous other proposals to make lynching a federal crime. Specifically, the Dyer Anti-Lynching Bill played an important role in the decline of lynchings following 1921. The Dyer Anti-Lynching Bill provided fines and imprisonment for persons convicted of lynching in federal courts and fines and penalties against states, counties, and towns which failed to use reasonable efforts to protect citizens from mob violence. The bill was passed by the House in 1922, but was killed in the Senate due to a filibuster of the Southern senators who claimed it would be unconstitutional and an infringement upon the states' rights. Even though the bill did not become law, it nevertheless influenced the decline of lynchings throughout the country.[20]

Despite all the equal rights and civil rights movements that were enacted in law, lynchings still occur today within the United States. While it is no longer as common a method of execution as it once was, there are still instances of lynchings for no other reason than the race or sexual preference of the victim. For instance, in 1998, Jerome Byrd was a black man who was lynched. He was dragged behind a pick-up truck until he eventually died. This man was accused of no crime other than being black.[21] Matthew Shephard was a young gay man, who, also in 1998, was brutally beaten, burned, and lashed to a fence in freezing weather to die. He died five days later of his injuries.[22] His death is considered a hate crime, but it could also be seen as a lynching, for what is the difference between what happened to Jerome Byrd and Matthew Shephard. They had committed no crime, but were killed simply because of some character they possessed. Today the United States hides behind the label *hate crime* where *lynching* was the common phrase of a century ago.

Armenia

One country that has experienced a violent history is Armenia. Armenia was the first country to accept Christianity as their state religion in 301 AD, and because of that has suffered years of persecution and conquest. In 1915–1916, the Young Turk Ottoman government carried out a great genocide against the Armenians until 1923. During this time, one and a half million Armenians were killed out of two and a half million that were part of the Ottoman Empire.[23]

The genocide was directed by a Special Organization established by the Committee of Union and Progress. This in turn created the "butcher battalions," which were made up of the most violent criminals released from prison. Any common Turk who attempted to protect an Armenian was killed. The Armenian genocide was committed in an orderly fashion, which proves it was orchestrated by the Young Turk government. The meticulous fashion of this orchestrated genocide proceeded as follows: First, the Armenian army was disarmed and placed into labor battalions. They were worked to death; killed by disease, hunger, or exposure; or were simply killed outright. Another method was they were bound and marched along isolated roads and systematically attacked by Kurdish tribesmen. Overall, approximately 200,000 Armenian soldiers are thought to have died this way.[24] Then, the Armenian political and intellectual leaders were gathered together on April 24, 1915, and were killed. Most who had been killed up to this point were men. Finally, those Armenians who remained, primarily the women and children, were herded out of their homes, were told they were to be relocated, and were marched to concentration camps in the desert where they subsequently died of starvation and thirst in the burning sun. Sometimes, instead of sending them into the desert, they would place them on barges and then sink them out at sea.[25] By 1923, a total of 2,102,000 Armenians were killed by the Young Turk government.[26]

Today, the Turkish government denies the allegations that these atrocities occurred, stating they were simply moving Armenians out of the "war zone." But the Armenian Genocide did not just occur in this "war zone" located in the eastern region, it occurred in all areas of the country. Despite the fact that the Turkish government denies these occurrences, there is no doubt about the reality. Even Hitler remarked years later on the genocide that occurred in Armenia, when he told his troops: "Go, kill without mercy . . . who today remembers the annihilation of the Armenians."[27] Hitler had seen how the Turks had eradicated the Armenian army and intelligentsia, while the rest of the world sat back and let it happen, and so he figured the same would hold true for the Germans and their desire to eliminate the

Jewish population, as well as all those who threatened the sovereignty of Hitler and his ideology.

On October 20, 2000, then President Clinton ordered Speaker of the House, J. Dennis Hastert, to shelve legislation that would have declared the mass killings of Armenians genocide. Today, Turkey is a key military ally of the United States, as well as a member of NATO, and President Clinton decided to put politics before historical accuracy.[28]

Even now there are still pockets of Armenians who continue to fear a future genocide. In the Autonomous Region of Mountainous Karabagh, also known as Nagorno-Karabagh, 77 percent of the population are Christian Armenians. Nagorno-Karabagh recently declared their independence from Azerbaijan because of their continued persecution, oppression, and human rights violations at the hands of the Azeri Turks. This region has been tossed back and forth between Armenia and Azerbaijan throughout the years. Because the area is made up of predominately Armenians, while under the control of Azerbaijan, the Azeri Turks constantly persecuted the Armenians in an attempt to drive them from the area and replace them with Azeris. The situation in Nagorno-Karabagh was first brought to the attention of the world in 1988 during Gorbachev's era of glasnost with a massive peaceful demonstration in Yerevan, the capital of Armenia. In fact, through this demonstration and other reform movements in the region, they ignited the independence movements in the rest of the Soviet Bloc of Eastern Europe. This small area is thus in part responsible for the fall of Communism, not only in Eastern Europe, but in the Soviet Union itself.[29]

But their surge for independence has not been easy, nor has it been peaceful. The Azeris have met this desire for independence with violence. There were multiple massacres of Armenian people between 1988 and 1990. Between 1990 and 1996, a war ensued when the Azeris began an outright military attack on the region of Nagorno-Karabagh. The Armenians were avidly protecting their homelands, and the Azeris were desperately trying to preserve their power over a foreign province. As of April 1996, there was a cease-fire, but it is tenuous at best. At any time the Azeris can begin another attack on the small region. A genocide similar to what occurred in 1915 is threatened unless outside countries become aware of the precarious position the Armenians in Nagorno-Karabagh are in, and lend aid and protection to the small group.[30]

China

The large number of deaths that occurred and continue to occur in China do not technically fall under genocide, although the government is completely responsible for the deaths of more than 38 million people between 1923 and 1987.

This includes over 15 million people who died in Chinese concentration camps. This number, though, does not include the 27,000,000 people who died from starvation because of Mao's agricultural mismanagement in the early 1960s. This famine was the worst in all of history and was caused entirely by the politicians, although not deliberately. Infanticide and coerced abortions are also the cause of a large number of children dying. Since 1971, over 110 million deaths have been estimated to be the result of coerced abortions and infanticide. These abortions are not always done with the consent of the parents, and are therefore deemed murder. While these types of deaths do not clearly fall under the UN's definition of genocide, an argument could be made for their inclusion because of both the role the government plays in these deaths and the intentional killing of a certain type of individual, in particular babies.[31]

Ukraine

Between 1932 and 1933, a man-made famine swept through the ethnic-Ukrainian region of the northern Caucasus and the lower Volga River. This famine was orchestrated by Joseph Stalin, the leader of the Soviet Union, and his henchman Lazar Kaganovich. The main purpose of this famine was to break the spirit of the peasant-farmers and force them into collectivism. Another goal of the famine was to stop the renaissance that was occurring in the Ukraine under the approval of the communist Ukrainian government. The Soviet government perceived this renaissance as a threat to "Russo-Centric Soviet" rule, and therefore proceeded to end it.[32]

This forced famine occurred because the Soviet's increased their grain quota for the region by 44 percent. This high percentage resulted in a grain shortage, and the people had to go without in order to meet the quota. Peasants who attempted to keep some of the grain were killed. In addition, an internal passport system was implemented, so that they were unable to move around the country in search of food. The grain was collected and stored in grain elevators in the same areas as the starving peasants and were protected by the army and secret police units. This deliberate act on the part of the Soviet government falls directly under Article II of the 1948 UN Genocide Convention, even though these acts occurred 16 years before the convention. Ultimately, between seven and ten million Ukrainians lost their lives that year.[33]

Soviet Union

The incident described above in the Ukraine was not the only time the Soviet Union was responsible for innocent people losing their lives due to the deliberate actions of the government. According to Rudolph Rummel, in his book *Death by Government*, the "Soviet Union exemplifies the dictum that government is a mechanism by which depraved people legitimize their depravity. As an all-powerful state, the Soviet government attracted the most depraved people who then unleashed the worst depravity. Stalin is unique only in surpassing all others in this regard." The death toll in the Soviet Union exceeded, nearly doubled, the number of people killed during all of the wars during the twentieth century.[34]

Other instances of the brutality of the Soviet Union's government can been seen during much of the first 50 years of the twentieth century. Millions of people were sent to gulags, Soviet concentration camps, where as many as 20 percent of all prisoners died. Many others suffered through the drug-torture of the "psychiatric hospitals," where resistence was legal proof for more "treatment." In 1919, hundreds of thousands of Don Cossacks were slaughtered in mass murders. During the 1930s, death quotas were issued by region for the Soviet secret police. Innocent people were killed for no other reason than to meet those quotas: mothers, children, boys. Between 1930 and 1937, 6,500,000 "kulaks," lower-middle-class peasants, were systematically murdered. From 1937 to 1938, approximately 1,000,000 Communists were murdered by Stalin during his Great Terror. Finally, in 1949, approximately 50,000–60,000 Estonians were deported and murdered. Overall, between 1919 and 1991, close to 62,000,000 people were killed at the hands and wishes of the Soviet government.[35]

Japan

The crimes of Japan involve the military invasion and massacring of millions of people in China, the Philippines, the Dutch East Indies, French Indochina, Singapore, Malaysia, and Burma. The majority of the crimes were committed in China against the innocent, and largely unarmed, Chinese population. The Japanese military caused destruction and terror throughout Asia from the time of their invasion of China in 1937 until their defeat by the United States in 1945. During this period, Japan was responsible for nearly 6,000,000 deaths, over half of which occurred in China. These numbers, however, do not include civilian deaths.[36] The Department of Defense of the Republic of China estimates that over 35,000,000 Chinese civilians were killed during this period of time.[37]

The Japanese military not only invaded China, but massacred their people. One such instance occurred on December 13, 1937, in the city of Nanjing, at that time the capital of China. This invasion occurred five days after the Chinese troops refused to surrender. The Nanjing Massacre, also known as the

Rape of Nanjing, lasted six weeks, in which approximately 300,000 Chinese soldiers and civilians were killed and 20,000 women were raped. During these six weeks, the Japanese killed unarmed civilians, raped, looted, burned, and committed mass executions.[38]

When the Japanese army entered the city of Nanjing, more than 100,000 refugees and injured soldiers crowded into the streets. The army opened fire on these crowds, killing indiscriminately. This lasted two days. The streets became "streets of blood" following this attack. Civilians were used as targets and practice "dummies" for the Japanese. There was no regard for human life. A complete annihilation ensued, not only of the citizens but also of the town itself. The Japanese burned the beautiful historical city of Nanjing to ashes.[39]

The Japanese have continued to deny this atrocity ever occurred, and the Chinese, as well as the rest of Asia affected and attacked by the Japanese army during World War II, have remained relatively quiet, allowing the war crimes of the Japanese to be largely forgotten.[40] If it had not been for the atomic bombing of Japan in 1945, the brutal acts by their military might have continued for much longer. These acts precariously fall under Article II of the 1948 UN Genocide Convention. It is hard to know exactly what provoked the Japanese military to act in such a barbaric fashion, and so it is difficult to determine if they acted with intent on destroying these groups of people. While it does appear they were "intent to destroy" select cities, it is hard to imagine the Japanese capable of destroying the entire Chinese population or culture. These acts could, though, be seen as pockets of genocide, with the Japanese military intending to destroy this particular city and all those who resided there at the time of their attack.

Germany

The Holocaust is possibly one of the worst atrocities of the twentieth century. It involved at least ten countries, and millions of lives were taken all because of whom they were, not because they had done anything wrong. These were not soldiers, they were civilians, caught in the crossfire of hatred and prejudice. The death rate in some small towns in Poland, Russia, and Lithuania was so high that only 1 in 100 people survived. The Holocaust affected the Jewish community predominately, although they were not the only group singled out for extermination. Gypsies and homosexuals were also targeted, millions losing their lives during this period in history.[41]

The Holocaust is the reason the term *genocide* was coined and the crime was addressed by the United Nations. Even though the Armenians faced a similar experience almost 30 years earlier, the crime was not identified until after World War II. During the Armenian "holocaust," the world remained silent regarding the brutality that occurred there. As noted earlier, Hitler was aware of this reaction by the world community and attempted to reenact the atrocities of the earlier crime. There is no written document ordering the SS, the private army of the Nazi party, to execute Jews; there was only an oral order given by Hitler, and it was followed without any dissent or public discussions. It is hard to believe the executions of approximately 6.5 million Jews occurred simply because one man ordered it to happen.[42]

This order by Hitler helped establish the definition of *genocide*. His intent was to destroy every vestige of the Jewish community, as well as other select groups. The Nazis did not just execute the Jews, they also tortured them. Jews, both in and out of concentration camps, lived in a constant state of terror. There was no reprieve, except death, and even up until the last minute of life, terror remained. They were demoralized, dehumanized, starved, beaten, and killed.[43] The Nazis also acted collectively; they had a collective responsibility, if one German was harmed, thousands of Jews were killed. The Jews were persecuted as a group, and therefore in order for them to resist, they had to act as a group.[44]

The military installed a code language in order to keep the Jews in the dark regarding their fate. Examples of this code are: resettlement—sending to the gas chambers; action—massacre; special treatment—gassing; pieces—victims; and showers—camouflaged gas chambers. This "code" constantly kept the Jews from knowing what was going to happen to them, and this only perpetuated the fear and terror they already felt. To add to the deception, the military sent postcards back to the family members who remained in the towns describing the move and their new "home." Usually by the time the postcards were received, the senders were already dead.[45]

One of the most "distinguishing" features, although not exclusive to the Holocaust, was the death camps, or concentration camps. The camps could hold up to 20,000 people per day. The gas chambers were masqueraded as bath houses, and the Jews were told they were being sent in to be disinfected. They were gathered together, and told to strip and place all valuables in the "windows" provided. Next, they were escorted to the "barber room," where they were shaved. They were then sent down an open-air corridor of 150 meters toward the "baths and inhalants." The Jews were told they were to breath in deeply because the inhalant would strengthen their lungs and prevent them from acquiring contagious diseases. But the smell of the room was obvious. The air ducts were connected to the tail-pipe of a Diesel truck. After all of the individuals were in the "bath house," the truck was turned on and the carbon monoxide was pumped into the room. This method of execution took more than thirty minutes. The bodies were then dumped in mass graves.[46]

Overall, approximately 21 million people were killed during the Holocaust. From 15,000,000 to over 31,600,000 people approximately were killed through the practice of genocide, which entailed the killing of hostages, reprisal raids, forced labor, "euthanasia," starvation, exposure, medical experiments, terror bombing, and in the concentration and death camps. The Nazi death machine is best known and ranks behind the Soviet Union and China for the most people murdered by their governments. But the Nazi's rank first in death rates among their populations during the brief six years when the majority of their killing occurred, which was when approximately 1 in 93 people were murdered per year by the Nazi regime in German occupied countries. While the Soviet Union and China executed more people, the Nazi regime crossed boundaries and limits of brutality rarely seen in the twentieth century.[47]

Poland and Eastern Europe

Following the fall of Nazi Germany, the crime of genocide did not cease. Instead, the countries previously occupied by the German army and persecuted by them turned the tables; those persecuted this time were the Germans. Similar to the method adopted by the Nazis, the Polish, Czech, Yugoslavians, and Russians rounded up innocent civilians, placed them in cattle cars, and shipped them off to concentration camps where they were tortured, murdered, or killed by the brutal conditions in which they were kept.[48]

The revenge that was carried out against the German civilians was severe. Nearly 2,000,000 Germans were killed during this ethnic cleansing that had as its stated goal the expulsion of ethnic Germans from Eastern Europe. Nearly 15,000,000 people are estimated to have been driven from their homes. Poland, who after the war contained a fourth of prewar Germany, had approximately 8,000,000 Germans within its borders. All were driven from their homes, and an estimated 1,500,000 were killed in the process. Almost 200,000 were killed in Czechoslovakia and 82,000 in Yugoslavia. This form of retribution, while understandable after their experiences at the hands of the Nazis, does not justify their actions and the additional killing of nearly 2,000,000 innocent people.[49]

Vietnam

In 1945, the Vietnamese Communists implemented a plan—to kill anyone who disagreed with them. The plan was carried out. Noncommunist politicians, sympathizers, and the friends, families, and co-workers of political enemies also were killed. Next the class of landlords were targeted. But the definition of *land-lord* was changed in order to apply the term to a larger number of individuals. *Landlord* now referred to anyone with an above-average income. This could be as simple as an extra cow. It also applied to anyone who at one time had an above-average income or had ancestors who had an above-average income at one time. The low income peasants were asked to identify these individuals and kill them. Eventually, the Communists set quotas per village—5 percent of the population of each village was to be killed. Between 1953 and 1956, approximately 150,000 people were killed to meet the quotas. Following these extermination processes, an additional 10,000 peasants were killed during a rebellion.[50]

Next, beginning in 1957, the Communists implemented a new plan—an extermination of all those who appeared to be capable of mobilizing support against them. This plan, then, was not only against those who spoke out against the government, but anyone who appeared capable of doing so. This eventually included teachers who failed to appear sympathetic to the government. An estimated six to seven thousand were killed under this plan. While that is not a very large number, it contained the leaders and the intelligentsia of the community.[51]

It was at this point that the United States got involved in the fight to protect the interests and people of South Vietnam. But during the U.S. involvement, the Communists did not stop the genocide; instead the number increased to involve anyone who was involved with anticommunist individuals, particularly Americans. The U.S. involvement led to tens of thousands of South Vietnamese being killed.[52]

A reign of terror also was implemented. Streets were mined and refugee camps were attacked. Neighborhood communities were shelled simply as a matter of policy with the goal of killing innocent citizens. With all the massive attacks on the civilians, approximately 164,000 innocents were killed. Groups of civilians were rounded up and shot for no apparent reason. Genocide was excessive in Vietnam because of the fear the Communists felt for those who disagreed with them.[53]

The killing did not end with South Vietnam's surrender in 1975. It continued, and another 160,000 people were killed. Following the Vietnam War, the country was invaded by Cambodia and China, adding to the number of Vietnamese lives lost. Concentration camps and forced evacuations caused an additional 143,000 to be murdered. The exact numbers of those who lost their lives in Vietnam are unknown, however, the crimes continue to exist, and the numbers continue to grow.[54]

Australia

Australia's form of genocide was different than other countries. They did not attempt to kill a set of people. Instead they had child-removal policies which consisted of removing, either by force or coercion, indigenous children from their families. These policies were in effect until 1970, and there appears to be long-lasting effects of these policies on the children taken. For instance, there appears to be a high rate of imprisonment and death among Aborigines in custody.[55] Nearly half of the 18–24 year old Aborigines have been arrested, which has become almost a rite of passage for most young Aboriginal men.[56]

The Australian government does finally admit to these policies, although they do not offer monetary compensation for the pain and suffering caused these children. The government does not, though, believe that their policies and actions constituted violations of human rights.[57] This violation of human rights constitutes genocide according to the 1948 UN Genocide Convention, Article II, section e, specifically defining *genocide* as "forcibly transferring children of the group to another group." This separation was solely based on their ethnicity. These children were stolen from their families, instilled with a repugnance for everything Aboriginal, and prepared to become the lowest level worker in a predominately white and prejudicial community. Many of these Aborigines still suffer from the legacy instilled by their government for the 28 years these policies existed. Many of the children removed from their families are now searching for them. These actions and policies represent systematic racial discrimination. While the policies did not authorize the killing of the Aboriginal children, they did attempt to integrate them into the mainstream society with the goal of eliminating their racial and cultural identity.[58] Genocide of any type should never happen, so while the Australian government did not attempt to kill the Aborigines, it committed violations of human rights because its goal was the elimination of their identity, which is also illegal.

Cambodia

Between 1975 and 1979, 1.5 to 2 million people died from starvation, overwork, torture, and execution. During the Khmer Rouge revolution, 20 percent of the whole Cambodian population—men, women, and children—were killed by state-organized violence. Like in Nazi Germany, Yugoslavia, and Rwanda, those in political power conspired with a total disregard of human life in order to produce repression, misery, and murder on a massive scale. Unlike other occurrences of genocide worldwide, the Cambodian genocide is unique because it went undocumented for a long period of time, and is only now beginning to be investigated.[59]

The difference between the Nazis and the Khmer Rouge is that the Nazis sent a select group of people to concentration camps, the Khmer Rouge sent everybody to concentration camps. In effect, the entire country became a concentration camp. In a matter of days, entire communities were uprooted. Those who were unable to move were shot. Individuals were told not to bring food or water, which caused many of the old and many of the young to die. Corpses lined the streets leading out of the cities. It has been estimated that over 400,000 individuals lost their lives in this evacuation process. The refugees were assigned to villages that turned into collective farms, known as "killing fields." Once they entered the villages, they were never allowed to leave.[60]

Within these villages, individuals did not exist. Everything was communal. Laughter and crying were not allowed, and people were not allowed to have names. Friends, mail, telegrams, newspapers, or radios were also forbidden. There was no communication between villages, either. The refugees had no access to doctors or medicine, books or personal property of any kind. There was no schooling or music, as well. Affection for one another was absolutely forbidden. A mother found hugging her child would then have to watch her child shot. Religion was also not allowed. Those who were religious faced death. Before the Khmer Rouge revolution, 40,000–60,000 Buddhist monks lived in Cambodia. Only 800 existed after four years. Half the Muslims were killed, and other religious minorities faced similar fates.[61]

The purpose of the revolution was to cleanse Cambodia ethnically. Approximately 200,000 Chinese, 150,000 Vietnamese, and 12,000 Thai were killed. If individuals had been exposed to Western thought, they were killed. People who spoke another language, dealt with foreigners, or had an education were killed. The intelligentsia, teachers, politicians, and doctors were killed. Even people who wore glasses were killed. There was no discrimination in who was eligible for death in Cambodia. There were no laws to follow, only orders. If the orders were broken, that individual could be killed.[62]

Political torture camps were established. Suspected conspirators were tortured until they told who their co-conspirators higher up in the party were. Thousands were killed at torture camps. Even torturers who failed to extract a confession before the individual died could be killed. Only 14 people are thought to have survived these camps.[63]

The Khmer Rouge proceeded to invade Vietnam in 1977, where they killed over 30,000 civilians. Vietnam responded in 1979 by invading Cambodia and establishing a puppet government. This new government still proceeded to kill 230,000 people, while the Khmer Rouge killed an additional 150,000 through guerilla actions throughout the 1980s.[64] The atrocities that occurred in Cambodia are not unique, but are extreme. The Nazis expanded their killing to include many countries, but always the same types of people; the Khmer Rouge, however, maintained their killing to within their borders, except for the one instance of invading Vietnam. They attempted to exterminate their entire country's population by including everybody in the concentration camps and lifting restrictions on who could be killed. They would even kill each other if an order was broken. These atrocities are unthinkable, and what is so hard to imagine is that they went completely unnoticed by the rest of the world until recently. Between 1970 and 1987, almost 4,000,000 Cambodians were killed.[65] That kind of blindness is what causes these acts to continue to occur.

East Timor

The invasion of East Timor occurred on December 7, 1975, by Indonesia after East Timor attempted to gain their independence from them. East Timor has suffered under occupation until recently. Starvation, disease, and forced migration claimed at least 100,000 lives during the first year of occupation. The military has used harsh tactics to force the people of East Timor to obey the laws of Indonesia. Some methods utilized by the military include forced migration, rape and forced sterilization, forced military service, torture, murder, and harassment. It has been estimated that at least one in every four East Timorese has lost their life during this struggle. This invasion and act of genocide is different than others that have occurred in the world during the twentieth century. In this instance, the United States, as well as Australia and Britain, have been compliant to this terror. The United States has even provided funding, training, and weapons to the Indonesian military. The "friendly" relationship between Indonesia and the United States is too important to risk losing.[66]

Every time independence seems like a possibility, violence flares up again. Paramilitary groups have begun to harass, murder, torture, and threaten the East Timorese in an attempt to make them approve of integration into Indonesia. While exact numbers on the number of people killed during the current outbreak of violence are unknown, the death toll appears to be at least in the hundreds, although the actual number is probably much higher. Tens of thousands have been forced from their homes, and approximately 40,000 live in "refugee camps" controlled by the military.[67]

Since then, a vote was taken in August of 1999 regarding the independence of East Timor. The vote was administered by the United Nations, and 78.5 percent of the voting population rejected the idea of remaining part of Indonesia. Authority over East Timor was transferred to the United Nations from Indonesia on October 25, 1999, and the UN Security Council established UNTAET as the transitional authority responsible for East Timor during this transition away from Indonesia. The Indonesian militia forces were finally forced out of East Timor in late September 1999, leaving behind a broken country, with no form of government left.[68]

Today, the Indonesians continue to harass the East Timorese refugees left within West Timor, Indonesia. The refugees are stuck in a position where if they choose to leave Indonesia and return to East Timor, they face the brutality of the militias who operate the refugee camps.[69] Hopefully, with the aid of the United Nations and the establishment of their transition government, East Timor will eventually be completely free of the terror and horror the Indonesians have inflicted on this country for years.

The crime of genocide occurs all over the world. From small countries, like Rwanda, to the United States, the desire to eliminate certain groups in a population exists. The United States is not exempt from that desire. Indians were victimized for years at the hands of the government, as they were evicted from their homes and sent to special "camps" to live. Massacres and disease also added to the crimes committed against this group of people. It has only been in the last several months that the government has finally apologized for the crimes of genocide they committed.[70]

Genocide is a crime that causes us to think of the Nazis in Germany or of Stalin in Russia, but rarely are these crimes thought to exist today as we begin the new millennium, but they do. It is time for these crimes to come to an end, and for that to happen, there can be no complacency when these crimes do occur. Too often, it seems, other countries look away from the crimes being committed, and until that comes to an end, the crime of genocide will always exist, and innocent people will continue to die at the hands of their governments.

Notes

1. Raphael Lemkin, *Rule in Europe*, 1944.

2. International Encyclopedia of the Social Science, vol. 7 (Macmillian and Free Press, 1968), 518.

3. Gerald Scully, *Murder by the State* (National Center for Policy Analysis, 1997).

4. Helen Fein, *Accounting for Genocide* (Free Press, 1979), 1.

5. Scully, *Murder by the State*, 2–3.

6. R. J. Rummel, draft table, *Statistics of Democide*, unpublished manuscript, 1993, 366–69. (all three tables).

7. http://www.spartacus.schoolnet.co.uk/USAlynching.htm.

8. Lynching–History. http://www.africana.com/Articles/tt_374.htm.

9. Lynching: http://www.berea.edu/ENG/chesnutt/lynching.html.

10. http://www.spartacus.schoolnet.co.uk/USAlynching.htm.

11. Lynching: http://www.berea.edu/ENG/chesnutt/lynching.html.

12. Robert A. Gibson, "The Negro Holocaust: Lynching and Race Riots in the United States, 1880–1950."

13. Lynching: http://www.berea.edu/ENG/chesnutt/lynchingstat.html.

14. Gibson, "The Negro Holocaust."

15. Lynching: http://www.spartacus.schoolnet.co.uk/USAlynching.htm.

16. Lynching: http://www.africana.com/Articles/tt_374.htm.

17. Gibson, "The Negro Holocaust."

18. Ibid.

19. Ibid.

20. Ibid.

21. Lynching: http://www.berea.edu/ENG/chesnutt/lynching.htm.

22. http://www.uwacadweb.uwyo.edu/lgbta/shephard.htm.

23. Armenian Research Center, Dearborn, Mich.–Fact Sheet: Armenian Genocide.

24. Freedom's Nest: Democide in Turkey.

25. Armenian Research Center, Dearborn, Mich.–Fact Sheet: Armenian Genocide.

26. Freedom's Nest: Democide in Turkey.

27. Ibid.

28. "Hostert Kills Bill on Turkey," *Chicago Sun-Times*, October 20, 2000.

29. Armenian Research Center, Dearborn, Mich.–Fact Sheet: Nagorno-Karabagh.

30. Ibid.

31. Freedom's Nest: Democide in Communist China.

32. The Artificial Famine/Genocide in Ukraine.

33. Ibid.

34. Freedom's Nest: Democide in the Soviet Union.

35. Ibid.

36. Ibid., Democide in Militarist Japan.

37. Nanjing Massacre and the Tokyo War Crimes Trial.

38. Ibid.

39. Ibid.

40. Ibid.

41. Holocaust Educational Digest: What Happened? and Other Genocides.

42. Ibid.: What Happened?; Who Ordered the Killings?; Who Organized the Holocaust?

43. Ibid., Terror and Starvation.

44. Ibid., Collective Responsibility.

45. Ibid., Deception and Hoaxes.

46. Ibid., Belzec–the worst death camp by A. Kimel.

47. Freedom's Nest: Democide in Nazi Germany.

48. Freedom's Nest: Democide in Poland and Eastern Europe.

49. Ibid.

50. Freedom's Nest: Democide in Vietnam.

51. Ibid.
52. Ibid.
53. Ibid.
54. Ibid.
55. Amnesty International Report–ASA 12/02/98 (summary).
56. Ibid., report.
57. Ibid., summary.
58. Ibid., report.
59. Cambodian Genocide Program at Yale.
60. Freedom's Nest: Cambodian Democide.
61. Ibid.
62. Ibid.
63. Ibid.
64. Ibid.
65. Ibid.
66. Jeffrey Benner, *Dossier: East Timor*, September 11, 1999.
67. Ibid.
68. Amnesty International–ASA 57/004/2000, AI index.
69. Ibid.
70. Matt Kelley, "U.S. Official Apologizes to Indians," *Washington Post*, September 9, 2000.

APPENDIX: CAPITAL PUNISHMENT STATISTICS

Table A.1
Countries That Have Abolished the Death Penalty for All Crimes[1]

Country	Date of Abolition for All Crimes	Date of Abolition for Ordinary Crimes	Date of Last Execution
Andorra	1990		1943
Angola	1992		
Australia	1985	1984	1967
Austria	1968	1950	1950
Azerbaijan	1998		1993
Belgium	1996		1950
Bermuda	1999		1977
Bulgaria	1998		1989
Cambodia	1989		
Canada	1998	1976	1962
Cape Verde	1981		1835
Columbia	1910		1909
Costa Rica	1877		
Croatia	1990		
Czech Republic[2]	1990		
Denmark	1978	1933	1950
Djibouti	1995		****
Dominican Republic	1966		
East Timor	1999		
Ecuador	1906		
Estonia	1998		1991
Finland	1972	1949	1944
France	1981		1977
Georgia	1997		1944*
Germany[3]	1987		
Greece	1993		1972
Guinea-Bissau	1993		1986*
Haiti	1987		1972*
Honduras	1956		1940
Hong Kong[4]	1993		
Hungary	1990		1988
Iceland	1928		1830
Ireland	1990		1954
Italy	1994	1947	1947
Kiribati			****
Liechtenstein	1987		1785

(continued)

Lithuania	1998		1995
Luxembourg	1979		1949
Macedonia	1991		
Marshall Islands			****
Mauritius	1995		1987
Micronesia			****
Moldova	1995		
Monaco	1962		1847
Mozambique	1990		1986
Namibia	1990		1988*
Nepal	1997	1990	1979
Netherlands	1982	1870	1952
New Zealand	1989	1961	1957
Nicaragua	1979		1930
Norway	1979	1905	1948
Palau			
Panama			1903*
Paraguay	1992		1928
Poland	1997		1988
Portugal	1976	1867	1849*
Romania	1989		1989
San Marino	1865	1848	1468*
Sao Tome and Principe	1990		****
Seychelles	1993		****
Slovak Republic	1990		
Slovenia	1989		
Solomon Islands		1966	****
South Africa	1997	1995	1991
Spain	1995	1978	1975
Sweden	1972	1921	1910
Switzerland	1992	1942	1944
Turkmenistan	1999		
Turvalu			****
Ukraine	1999		
United Kingdom	1998	1973	1964
Uruguay	1907		
Vanuatu			****
Vatican City State	1969		
Venezuela	1863		

*Date of last *known* execution.
****No executions since independence.

Table A.2
Countries That Have Abolished the Death Penalty for Ordinary Crimes Only[5]

Country	Date of Abolition for Ordinary Crimes	Date of Last Execution
Albania[6]	1999	1995
Argentina	1984	
Bolivia	1997	1974
Bosnia-Herzegovina	1997	
Brazil	1979	1855
Cook Islands		
Cyprus	1983	1962
El Salvador	1983	1962*
Fiji	1979	1964
Israel	1954	1962
Latvia[7]	1999	1996
Malta	1971	1943
Mexico		1937
Peru	1979	1979

*Date of last *known* execution.

Table A.3
Countries That Retain the Death Penalty but Are Abolitionist in

Country	Date of Last Execution
Bhutan	1964*
Brunei Darussalam	1957*
Central African Republic	1988
Congo (Republic)	1982
Côte d'Ivoire	
Gambia	1981
Grenada	1978
Madagascar	1958*
Maldives	1952*
Mali	1980
Nauru	****
Niger	1976*
Papua New Guinea	1950
Samoa	****
Senegal	1967
Sri Lanka	1976
Suriname	1982
Togo	
Tonga	1982
Turkey	1984

*Date of last *known* execution.
****No executions since independence.

Table A.4
Countries That Retain and Use the Death Penalty for Ordinary Crimes[9]

Afghanistan	Liberia
Algeria	Libya
Antigua and Barbuda	Malawi
Armenia	Malaysia
Bahamas	Mauritania
Bahrain	Mongolia
Bangladesh	Morocco
Barbados	Myanmar
Belarus	Nigeria
Belize	North Korea
Benin	Oman
Botswana	Pakistan
Burundi	Palestinian Authority
Cameroon	Philippines
Chad	Qatar
Chile	Russian Federation
China	Rwanda
Comoros	St. Christopher & Nevis
Congo (Democratic Republic)	Saint Lucia
Cuba	Saint Vincent & Grenadines
Domina	Saudi Arabia
Egypt	Sierra Leone
Equatorial Guinea	Singapore
Eritrea	Somalia
Ethiopia	South Korea
Gabon	Sudan
Ghana	Swaziland
Guatemala	Syria
Guinea	Taiwan
Guyana	Tajikistan
India	Tanzania
Indonesia	Thailand
Iran	Trinidad & Tobago
Iraq	Tunisia
Jamaica	Uganda
Japan	United Arab Emirates
Jordan	United States of America
Kazakstan	Uzbekistan
Kenya	Vietnam
Kuwait	Yemen
Kyrgyzstan	Yugoslavia (Federal Republic)
Laos	Zambia
Lebanon	Zimbabwe
Lesotho	

Table A.5
Crimes Punishable by Death[10]

Country	Crimes Punishable by Death
Belize	Criminal homicide
China	68 capital offenses including: Offenses related to national security Setting fires, breaking dikes, etc., leading to serious injuries or death Intentional murder Rape Robbery Theft Fraud Corruption
Cuba	In February 1999, expanded scope of crimes punishable by death to include serious cases of drug trafficking, corruption of minors, and armed robbery.
Egypt	A crime associated with terrorist activity that results in the loss of life Drug trafficking Apostasy of a Muslim Rape Murder
Ghana	Murder Armed robbery Conspiracies against the government
India	Murder Drug trafficking Kidnapping
Iran	Drug trafficking Armed robbery Murder Incest Rape Sex between a non-Muslim and a Muslim female Adultery Sodomy Homosexual acts after a fourth conviction Drinking liquor after a prior conviction Drawing arms to create fear or intimidation and to destroy the freedom and security of the people

(continued)

	Membership in banned organization, e.g., the Bahai faith Plotting against the government
Iraq	Counter revolutionary activity Drug trafficking Murder Rape Sex between a non-Muslim and a Muslim female
Japan	14 capital offenses including: Murder Robbery Espionage and treason Terrorist activity that results in death
Kenya	Murder Treason
Malaysia	Murder Armed robbery Treason Currency offenses Embezzlement of public funds
Nigeria	Murder Armed robbery Conspiracies against the government Arson Tampering with oil pipelines, importing or exporting mineral ore or oil without authority, tampering with electric or telephone cables, dealing in petroleum products without a license
Oman	In April 2000, expanded scope of crimes punishable by death to include drug-related crimes.
Russia	According to the new Constitution of 1993, a capital sentence may be imposed only for serious violent offenses against human life.
Saudi Arabia	Rebellion Highway robbery involving homicide Adultery Premeditated murder if the victim's family seeks retaliation Espionage

(continued)

Table A.5 *(Continued)*
Crimes Punishable by Death

Country	Crimes Punishable by Death
	Sodomy
	Sabotage (including the destruction of homes, public buildings, water and resources, and aircrafts)
	Drug trafficking
	Armed robbery
	Apostasy from Islam
Sierra Leone	Murder
	Coup attempts
Singapore	Discretionary death sentences for 7 offenses
	Mandatory death sentences for:
	Murder
	Treason
	Certain firearm offenses
	Trafficking in certain drugs
Ukraine	Aggravated homicide
	Rape of a minor
	Treason
	Espionage
	Some military offenses
United Arab Emirates	In October 1999, expanded scope of crimes punishable by death to include importing banned material or nuclear waste and dumping or storing such materials inside the country.
United States of America[11]	Murder
	Rape of a child (only in certain jurisdictions)
	Kidnapping (only in certain jurisdictions)
	Terrorist activities (federal law)
Vietnam	20 capital offenses including:
	Drug offenses
	Murder
	Rape
	Corruption and fraud (when the sums involved are over a certain amount)
Zimbabwe	Murder
	Treason

Table A.6
Methods of Execution Provided by Law

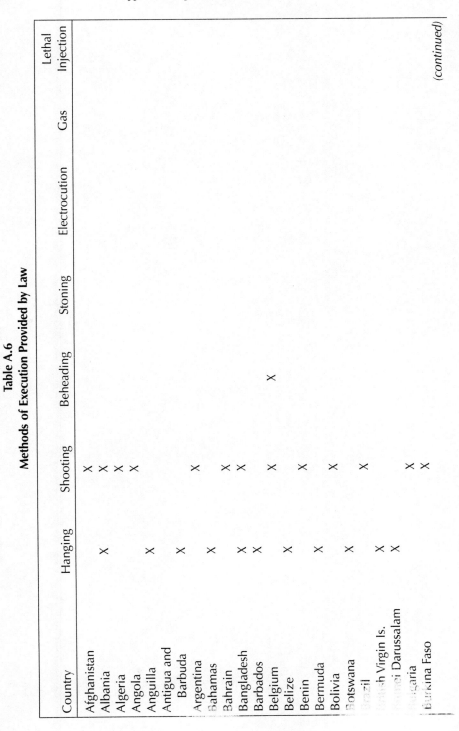

Country	Hanging	Shooting	Beheading	Stoning	Electrocution	Gas	Lethal Injection
Afghanistan		X					
Albania	X	X					
Algeria		X					
Angola		X					
Anguilla	X						
Antigua and Barbuda	X						
Argentina		X					
Bahamas	X						
Bahrain		X					
Bangladesh	X	X					
Barbados	X	X					
Belgium	X	X	X				
Belize	X	X					
Benin		X					
Bermuda	X	X					
Bolivia		X					
Botswana	X	X					
Brazil		X					
British Virgin Is.	X						
Brunei Darussalam	X						
Bulgaria		X					
Burkina Faso		X					

(continued)

**Table A.6 *(Continued)*
Methods of Execution Provided by Law**

Country	Hanging	Shooting	Beheading	Stoning	Electrocution	Gas	Lethal Injection
Burma	X						
Burundi	X	X					
Cameroon	X	X					
Canada		X					
Cayman Is.	X						
Central African Rep.		X					
Chad		X					
Chile		X					
China		X					
Comoros		X					
Congo		X	X				
Cote d'Ivoire		X					
Cuba		X					
Cyprus	X						
Czechoslovakia	X	X					
Djibouti		X					
Dominica	X						
Egypt	X	X					
El Salvador		X					
Equatorial Guinea	X	X					
Ethiopia	X	X					
Fiji	X						
Gabon		X					

(continued)

Gambia	X		
Ghana		X	
Greece		X	
Grenada	X		
Guatemala		X	
Guinea		X	
Guinea-Bissau		X	
Guyana	X		
Hong Kong	X	X	
Hungary	X	X	
India	X	X	
Indonesia		X	
Iran	X	X	
Iraq	X	X	
Ireland	X	X	
Israel	X		
Italy		X	
Jamaica	X	X	
Japan	X	X	
Jordan	X		
Kampuchea		X	
Kenya			
Korea (Democratic People's Republic)	X		X

Appendix: Capital Punishment Statistics

Table A.6 (Continued)
Methods of Execution Provided by Law

Country	Hanging	Shooting	Beheading	Stoning	Electrocution	Gas	Lethal Injection
Korea (Republic)	X	X					
Kuwait	X	X					
Lebanon	X	X					
Lesotho	X						
Liberia	X	X					
Libya	X	X					
Madagascar		X					
Malawi	X						
Malaysia	X						
Mali		X					
Mauritania		X	X	X			
Mauritius	X						
Mexico		X					
Montserrat	X						
Morocco		X					
Mozambique		X					
Namibia	X						
Nepal	X	X					
New Zealand	X						
Niger		X					
Nigeria	X	X		X			
Pakistan	X						
Papua New Guinea	X						

Country				
Paraguay		X		
Peru	X	X		
Poland	X	X		
Qatar		X	X	
Romania		X		
Rwanda		X		
St. Christopher and Nevis	X			
St. Lucia	X			
St. Vincent and the Grenadines	X	X		
Saudi Arabia			X	X
Senegal	X	X		
Sierra Leone	X	X		
Singapore		X		
Somalia	X			
South Africa	X	X		
Spain	X	X		
Sri Lanka	X	X		
Sudan	X	X		X
Suriname		X		
Swaziland	X	X		
Switzerland		X		
Syria	X	X		

(continued)

Table A.6 (Continued)
Methods of Execution Provided by Law

Country	Hanging	Shooting	Beheading	Stoning	Electrocution	Gas	Lethal Injection
Taiwan		X					
Tanzania	X						
Thailand		X					
Togo		X					
Tonga	X						
Trinidad and Tobago	X						
Tunisia	X	X					
Turkey	X						
Turks and Caicos Is.	X						
Uganda	X	X					
USSR	X	X					
United Arab Emirates		X	X	X			
United Kingdom	X						
USA	X	X			X	X	X
Vietnam		X					
Western Samoa		X					
Yemen (Arab Republic)		X	X	X			
Yemen (People's Democratic Republic)		X					
Yugoslavia		X					
Zaire	X	X					
Zambia	X						
Zimbabwe	X						
Total No. of Countries	77	87	7	7	1	1	1

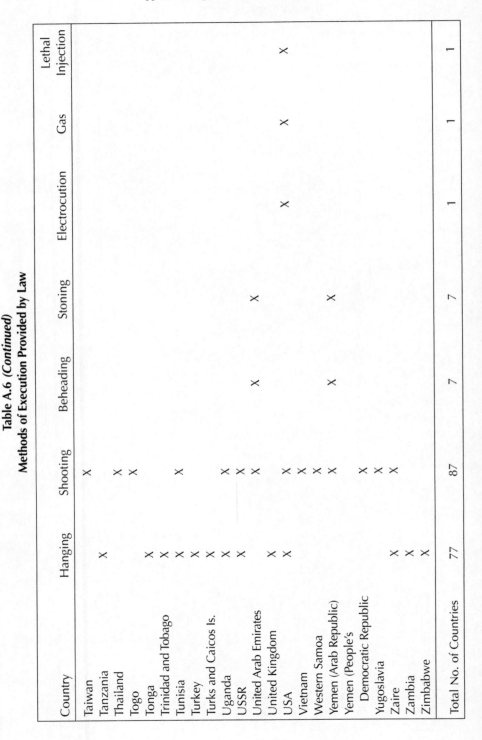

Table A.7
Recorded Worldwide Executions by Year, 1980–1999[12]

Year	Number of Countries Carrying Out Executions	Number of Executions Recorded	Number of Countries with over 100 Executions	% of All Recorded Executions Carried Out in Countries with over 100 Executions
1980	29	1,229		
1981	34	3,278		
1982	42	1,609		
1983	39	1,399		
1984	40	1,513	4	78
1985	44	1,125	3	66
1986	39	743	3	56
1987	39	769	3	59
1988	35	1,903	3	83
1989	34	2,229	3	85
1990	26	2,029	4	84
1991	32	2,086	2	89
1992	35	1,708	2	82
1993	32	1,831	1	77
1994	37	2,331	3	87
1995	41	3,276	3	85
1996	39	4,272	4	92
1997	40	2,607	3	82
1998	37	2,258	2	72
1999	31	1,813	4	80

Table A.8
Executions of Child Offenders, January 1990–December 1999[13]

Country	Name of Prisoner	Age at Time of Offense	Age at Time of Execution	Date of Execution
Iran	Kazem Shirafkan		17	1990
Iran	young male		16	9/29/92
Iran	young male		17	9/29/92
Iran	young male		17	9/29/92
Iran	Ebrahim Qobanzadeh		17	10/24/99
Nigeria	Chiebore Onuoha	15	17	7/31/97
Pakistan	Juvenile		17	11/15/92
Pakistan	Shamun Masih	14	23	9/23/97
Saudi Arabia	Sadeq Mal-Allah		17	9/3/92
USA	Dalton Prejean	17		5/18/90
USA	Johnny Garrett	17		2/11/92
USA	Curtis Harris	17		7/1/93
USA	Frederick Lashley	17		7/28/93
USA	Christopher Burger	17		12/7/93
USA	Ruben Cantu	17		8/24/93
USA	Joseph John Cannon	17		4/22/98
USA	Robert Anthony Carter	17		5/18/98
USA	Dwayne Allen Wright	17		10/14/98
USA	Sean Sellers	16		2/4/99
Yemen	Nasser Munir Nasser al'Kirbi		13	7/21/93

Table A.9
Number of Abolitionist Countries at Year End, 1981–1999[14]

Year	Number of Countries Abolitionist for All Crimes	Number of Countries Abolitionist in Law or Practice
1981	27	63
1982	28	63
1983	28	64
1984	28	64
1985	29	64
1986	31	66
1987	35	69
1988	35	80
1989	39	84
1990	46	88
1991	46	83
1992	50	84
1993	57	90
1994	55	96
1995	59	101
1996	60	100
1997	64	102
1998	70	105
1999	73	108

Notes

1. Amnesty International, July 2000.

2. The death penalty was abolished in the Czech and Slovak Federal Republic in 1990. On January 1, 1993, the Federal Republic divided into two states: the Czech Republic and the Slovak Republic. The last execution in the Czech and Slovak Federal Republic was in 1988.

3. The death penalty was abolished in the Federal Republic of Germany (FRG) in 1949 and in the German Democratic Republic (GDR) in 1987. The last execution in the FRG was in 1949; the date of the last execution in the GDR is not known. The FRG and the GDR were unified in October 1990.

4. In 1997, Hong Kong was returned to Chinese rule as a special administrative region of China. Amnesty International understands that Hong Kong will remain abolitionist.

5. Amnesty International, July 2000.

6. As of 1999, the death penalty in Albania can only be imposed in times of war or when war is imminent.

7. After ratifying the European Convention on Human Rights in 1999, Latvia became abolitionist with regard to crimes committed in peacetime.

8. Amnesty International, July 2000.

9. Amnesty International, July 2000.

10. Amnesty International, July 2000.

11. Twelve states and the District of Columbia do not impose the death penalty.

12. Amnesty International, *The Death Penalty Worldwide: Developments in 1999,* April 2000.

13. Amnesty International, *The Death Penalty Worldwide: Developments in 1999,* April 2000.

14. Amnesty International, *The Death Penalty Worldwide: Developments in 1999,* April 2000.

Bibliography

Alaska Justice Forum, Justice Center Publication, Spring 1999, Vol. 16, No. 1.

Amnesty International: ACT 50/011/1998, November 1998. *Juveniles and the Death Penalty: Executions Worldwide since 1990.* http://www.web.amnesty.org/ai.nsf/index/ACT500111998.

Amnesty International: ASA 20/031/1999, 01/18/1999. *India: An Appeal against Death Sentences.*

Amnesty International: ASA 57/004/2000–News Service Nr. 162. 29 August 2000. *East Timor: UNTAET, Justice and Refugees One Year after the Ballot.*

Amnesty International: The Death Penalty: List of Abolitionist and Retentionist Countries, Revised 18 December 1999. http://www.amnesty.org/ailib/intcam/dp/abrelist.htm

Amnesty International: *Death Penalty March 2000 News.* ACT 53/001/2000.

Amnesty International: *The Death Penalty Worldwide: Developments in 1999.* April 2000.

Amnesty International: July 2000.

Amnesty International: *People's Republic of China,* 1997. http://www.amnesty.org/ailib/intcam/dp/country/hard.htm.

Amnesty International–Report–AFR 01/03/97, April 1997. *Africa: A New Future without the Death Penalty.* http://www.amnesty.org/ailib/aipub/1997/AFR/10100397.htm.

Amnesty International–Report–ASA 03/01/97, January 1997. *Southeast Asia: Against the Tide: The Death Penalty in Southeast Asia.* http://www.amnesty.org/ailib/aipub/1997/ASA/30300197.htm.

Amnesty International–Report–ASA 12/02/98, (summary). *Silence on Human Rights: Government Responds to "Stolen Children" Inquiry.* http://www.web.amnesty.org/ai.nsf/index/ASA120021998.

Amnesty International Report–ASA 33/10/96, September 1996. *Pakistan: The Death Penalty.* http://www.amnesty.org/ailib/aipub/1996/ASA/33301096.htm.

Amnesty International Report: *Chile: A Human Rights Review Based on the International Covenant on Civil and Political Rights.* 01/07/1999. http://www.amnesty.org

Amnesty International–Report–EUR 57/10/96, July 1996. *Kazakstan: Ill-Treatment and the Death Penalty: A Summary of Concerns.* http://www.amnesty.org/ailib/aipub/1996/EUR/45701096.htm.

Amnesty International–*Saudi Arabia: Defying World Trends*; 12/06/2000–*Saudi Arabia: A Secret State of Suffering*, 27 March 2000. http://www.amnesty.org/ai.nsf/Index–search Death Penalty.

Amnesty International. *Silence on Human Rights: Government Responds to "Stolen Children" Inquiry*, March 1998. http://www.oneworld.org/guides/genocide/index.html.

Amnesty International USA Annual Report 1999: Chile, Belize, Colombia, Saudi Arabia, Iran. http://www.amnestyusa.org/ailib/aireport/ar99/.

Amnesty International. "USA: Increasing Concern over Execution of the Innocent." *Death Penalty News*, June 2000.

Amnesty International: Website against the Death Penalty–Facts and Figures on the Death Penalty. http://www.web.amnesty.org/rmp/dpl.

The Artificial Famine/Genocide in Ukraine. http://209.82.14.226/history/famine/.

Bailey, William. "Deterrence, Brutalization and the Death Penalty: Another Examination of Oklahoma's Return to Capital Punishment." *Criminology* 36, 1998.

Bailey, William C., and Ruth D. Peterson. "Murder, Capital Punishment and Deterrence: A Review of the Literature." Pp. 143 in *The Death Penalty in America: Current Controversies*, edited by Hugo Adam Bedau. Publisher, 1997.

Barnes, Harry Elmer. *Story of Punishment: A Record of Man's Inhumanity.* Patterson Smith Publishing Corporation, 1996.

Benner, Jeffery. *Dossier: East Timor–A Relatively Painless Primer on the History of the Conflict in East Timor*, September 11, 1999. http://www.ess.uwe.ac.uk/Timor/background2.htm.

Cambodian Genocide Program at Yale. http://www.yale.edu/cgp/main.htm.

The Campaign to End Genocide. http://www.endgenocide.org/aboutgen.html; http://www.endgenocide.org/text.html; http://www.endgenocide.org/definition.html.

"The Case for Innocence." *Frontline.* Interview of Barry Scheck.

Conners, Edward, Thomas Lundregan, Neal Miller, and Tom McEwen. "Convicted by Juries, Exonerated by Science: Case Studies in the Use of DNA Evidence to Establish Innocence after Trial." U.S. Department of Justice, Office of Justice Programs, June 1996.

Death Penalty Information Center. http://www.deathpenaltyinfo.org/dpicintl.html; http://www.deathpenaltyinfo.org/DRUSA-ExecUpdate.html; http://www.deathpenaltyinfo.org/dpicmr.html (mental health); http://www.deathpenaltyinfo.org/juvchar.html (juveniles).

"The Death Penalty on Trial." *Newsweek*, June 4, 2000.

Death Penalty USA Pages. http://www.agitator.com/dp/methods/index.html.

Death Penalty: When Life Generates Death (Legally). http://library.thinkquest.org/23685/data/eindex.html.

"Death Row Justice Derailed" (first of a five-part series). *Chicago Tribune*, November 14, 1999.

"The Dentist Takes the Stand." *Newsweek*, August 20, 2001.

Drapkin, Israel. *Crime and Punishment in the Ancient World*. Lexington Books, 1986.

Fact Sheet: Armenia; University of Michigan–Dearborn. http://www.umd.umich.edu/dept/armenian/facts/armenia.html; http://www.umd.umich.edu/dept/armenian/facts/genocide.html; http://www.umd.umich.edu/dept/armenian/facts/karabagh.html.

Fein, Helen. *Accounting for Genocide*. Free Press, 1979.

Forst, Brian. "Capital Punishment and Deterrence: Conflicting Evidence," *Journal of Criminal Law and Criminology* 74, fall 1983.

Freedom's Nest: from Rummel's book *Death By Government*. http://www.freedomsnest.com/rummel_murderers.html; http://www.freedomsnest.com/rummel_estimate.html; http://www.freedomsnest.com/rummel_totals.html.

Gallup International Millennium Survey. http://www.gallup-international.com

Genocide: Definitions and Controversies, University of the West of England. http://www.es.uwe.ac.uk/genocide/gendef.htm.

Genocide Resources: Links 2; University of Memphis and the Pennsylvania State University. http://www.people.memphis.edu/~genocide/link2.htm.

Gibson, Robert A. "The Negro Holocaust: Lynching and Race Riots in the United States, 1880–1950." Yale-New Haven Teachers Institute. http://www.yale.edu/ynhti/curriculum/units/1979/2/79.02.04.x.html.

Harries, Keith, and Derral Cheatwood. *The Geography of Execution: The Capital Punishment Quagmire in America*. Rowman & Littlefield Publishers, Inc., 1997.

"Hastert Kills Bill on Turkey." *Chicago Sun-Times*, October 20, 2000.

Holocaust Educational Digest: What Happened? and Other Genocides. http://users.systec.com/kimel/what.html.

Holocaust Educational Digest: What Happened?; Who Ordered the Killings?; Who Organized the Holocaust? http://users.systec.com/kimel/digest.html.

"Homicide and the Death Penalty." *Journal of Criminal Law and Criminology* 74, no. 3, 1983.

Hood, Roger. *The Death Penalty: A Worldwide Perspective*. Clarendon Press, 1996.

House, H. Wayne and John Howard Yoder. *The Death Penalty Debate: Issues of Christian Conscience*. Word Publishing, 1991.

Holy Bible, Catholic edition.

Huff, C. Ronald, Aryee Rattner, and Edward Sagarin. *Convicted But Innocent: Wrongful Conviction and Public Policy*. Sage Publications, Inc., 1996.

International Encyclopedia of the Social Sciences. Vol. 7 Macmillian and Free Press, 1968.

Johnson, Robert. *Death Work: A Study of the Modern Execution Process*. 2nd edition. Wadsworth Publishing Company, 1998.

Kelley, Matt. "U.S. Official Apologizes to Indians." *Washington Post*, September 9, 2000.

Kimel, Alexander. *Holocaust–Understanding and Prevention*, June 2000. http://users.systec.com/kimel/index.html#top.

Lemkin, Raphael. *Rule in Europe*. Publisher, 1944.

Library of Congress Country Studies: Chile, Belize, Columbia, Saudi Arabia, India. http://lcweb2.loc.gov/frd/cs/cshome.html.

"Life Unworthy of Life" Killing Programmes. http://www.ess.uwe.ac.uk/genocide/mord.htm.

Lynching: http://www.spartacus.schoolnet.co.uk/USAlynching.htm.

Lynching: http://www.berea.edu/ENG/chesnutt/lynching.html.

Lynching–History: http://www.africana.com/Articles/tt_374.htm.

Masur, Louis P. *Rites of Execution: Capital Punishment and the Transformation of American Culture, 1776–1865.* Oxford University Press, 1989.

Message Supporting the Moratorium on the Death Penalty. http://www.engaged-zen.org/HHDLMSG.html.

NACDL Death Penalty Defense. http://www.criminaljustice.org/DEATH/crinfo.htm.

Nanjing Massacre and the Tokyo War Crimes Trial. http://www.cnd.org/njmassacre/nj.html.

Radelet, Michael, and Hyo Adam Bedau. "The Execution of the Innocent." *Law and Contemporary Problems* 61, Autumn 1998.

Reggio, Michael H. History of the Death Penalty, 1999. http://www.tibf.co.uk/historydp.htm.

Rummel, R. J. *Statistics of Democide.* Unpublished manuscript, draft tables. 1993.

Scully, Gerald. *Murder by the State.* National Center for Policy Analysis, 1997.

Shephard, Matthew: http://www.geocities.com/WestHollywood/Stonewall/2878/index.html.

Simon, Rita J. *Public Opinion in America: 1936–1970.* Rand McNally, 1973.

Sorenson, John, and Robert Wrinkle, Victoria Brewer, and James Marquet. "Capital Punishment and Deterrence: Examining the Effect of Execution on Murder in Texas." *Crime and Delinquency* 45, 1999.

Sourcebook of Criminal Justice Statistics Online. http://www.albany.edu/sourcebook/1995/pdf/t681.pdf.

Statistical Abstract of the United States, 1995. http://www.census.gov/prod/www/statistical-abstract-us.html.

Study Finds Homicide Increase Faster during Periods of Executions, 4/21/95. http://www.prisonactivist.org/death-penalty/dpstudy.html.

Uniform Crime Reports: Crime in the United States, 1995. http://www.fbi.gov/ucr/95cius.htm.

U.S. Department of Justice, Bureau of Justices Statistics. http://www.ojp.usdoj.gov/bjs/pub/pdf/dcfacts.pdf. Capital Punishment Statistics: http://www.ojp.usdoj.gov/dbs/cp.htm.

U.S. News & World Report. Written by Joseph Shapiro. November 9, 1998.

Washington Post/ABC News poll. April 2001.

World Factbook of Criminal Justice Systems: http://www.ojp.usdoj.gov/bjs/abstract/wfcj.htm. Australia by David Biles, Australian Institute of Criminology. Canada by Debra Cohen and Sandra Longtin, State University of New York at Albany. England and Wales by Corretta Phillips, Rutgers University; Gemma Cox, University of Manchester; Ken Pease, University of Huddersfield. France by Jacques Borricand, Institut de Sciences Penales et de Criminologie. Germany by Alexis A. Aronowitz,

Netherlands Ministry of Justice. Italy by Peitro Marongiu, University of Cagliari; Mario Biddau, Corte d'Appello di Cagliara. Russia by Ilya V. Nikiforov. Poland by Andrzej Adamski, Nicolas Copernicus University. Slovenia by Alenka Selih and Darko Maver, University of Ljubljana. Ukraine by Sergey S. Chapkey, National Institute of Justice; Vladimir Tochilovsky, International Tribunal for the Former Yugoslavia. Czech Republic by Otakar Osmancik, Institut Pro Kriminologii a Socialni Prevenci. Slovak Republic by Maria Hencovska, Pavol Jozef Safarik University. Ghana, Kenya, and Nigeria by Obi N. I. Ebbe, State University of New York at Brockport. South Africa by Wilfried Scharf and Rona Cochrane, University of Cape Town. Israel by Gloria M. Weisman, Israeli Ministry of Justice. India by R. K. Raghavan, Indian Police Service. China by Jiana Guo, Ministry of Justice; Guo Ziang, China University of Politics and Law; Wu Zongxian, Ministry of Justice of China; Xu Zhangrun, Li Shuangshuang, University of Politics and Law. Japan by Tadashi Moriyama, Takushoku University. Singapore by Mahesh Nalla, Michigan State University.

Index

Page references followed by *t* and *n* indicate tables and notes, respectively.

About the Authors

Rita J. Simon is a Sociologist who earned her doctorate at the University of Chicago in 1957. Before coming to American University in 1983 to serve as dean of the School of Justice, she was a member of the faculty at the University of Illinois, at the Hebrew University on Jerusalem, and the University of Chicago. She is currently a "University Professor" in the School of Public Affairs and the Washington College of Law at American University.

Professor Simon has authored 26 books and edited 15 including: *In Their Own Voices* with Rhonda Roorda (2000); *Adoption Across Borders* with Howard Alstein (2000); *In the Golden Land: A Century of Russian and Soviet Jewish Immigration* (1997); *The Ambivalent Welcome: Media Coverage of American Immigration* with Susan Alexander (1993); *New Lives: The Adjustment of Soviet Jewish Immigrants in the United States and Israel* (1985); *Women's Movements in America Their Achievements, Disappointments, and Aspirations* with Gloria Danzinger (1986); *Rabbis, Lawyers, Immigrants, Thieves; Women's Roles in America* (1993); *Continuity and Change: A Study of Two Ethnic Communities in Israel* (1978); *The Crimes Women Commit, The Punishments They Receive* with Jean Landis (1991); *Adoption, Race and Identity* with Howard Alstein (1992); *The Case for Transracial Adoption* with Howard Altstein and Marygold Melli (1994).

She is currently editor of *Gender Issues*. From 1978 to 1981, she served as editor of *The American Sociological Review* and from 1983 to 1986 as editor of *Justice Quarterly*. In 1966, she received a Guggenheim Fellowship.

Since 1993, Professor Simon has served as president of the Women's Freedom Network.

Dagny Blaskovich received her Bachelor of Arts in the Program of Liberal Studies from the University of Notre Dame in 1998. Ms. Blaskovich went on to receive a Master's of Science in Justice, Law and Society from American University in Washington, D.C., in 2000. She is now currently working for the Chicago Police Department.